MOUNTAINTOP PROSPERITY

Move Quickly to New Heights
in Life, Work and Money

By

DAPHNE MICHAELS

ADITI

Printed in the United States of America.
First Printing: August 2016

ISBN 978-0-9914689-2-8

Disclaimer and Clarification:
The stories and examples included in this book are fictional composites based on the author's consulting and working experience with people for over twenty years. All names and any identifying details have been changed to protect the privacy of anyone referenced in this book.

Note to the reader:
This book is not intended as a substitute for the medical advice of physicians or for mental health diagnosis or treatment. The reader should regularly consult a physician or mental health professional in matters relating to his/her health and wellbeing and particularly with respect to any symptoms that may require professional diagnosis, therapeutic attention or treatment.

Neither the publisher nor the author is engaged in rendering professional advice or services to the individual reader. Any ideas, procedures, or suggestions contained in this book are not intended as a substitute for consulting with a physician. Neither the publisher nor the author shall be liable or responsible for any loss or damage allegedly arising from any information or suggestion in this book.

This book is dedicated to
Bruce McAllister
for meeting me at the mountaintop

Contents

Introduction 7

PART I
Understanding Mountaintop Prosperity

1 Consider Your Goals 13
2 Avoid Mountaintop Dead Ends 25
3 Breakthroughs—Eight Steps to the Mountaintop 31

PART II
Emerging Above the Fog

4 Meet Your Great Latent Self 45
5 Develop Mountaintop Thinking 53
6 Persist Through Challenges 61
7 Develop a Triumphant Approach 69
8 Stoke the Fire in Your Belly 79

PART III
Living Mountaintop Prosperity

9 Surrender to the Highest Good 89
10 Cultivate Your Courage to Love 95
11 Embrace the World 103

PART IV
Support for Your Climb

12 Mountaintop Prosperity Workbook 109

Acknowledgments 206
About the Author / Forthcoming Books 207

Introduction

When I was young, I had an experience that led me to understand two vast human worlds in terrible contrast: one of love and one of despair. Because I grew up on acres of land in the Pacific Northwest, my horse, Coco, was just steps outside my childhood home. He was always eager for me to ride him through the natural terrain, complete with a waterfall, green pasture, and forested trails. I cannot think of a life more pure and elegant than I experienced riding Coco. The world of love surrounded us in a cocoon of fresh air and singing birds. In this sense my childhood was a living paradise.

Too soon, by the age of eleven, the world of despair crept into my awareness. Its misery, greed, and violence were a shock to my spirit. I began to recognize darkness lurking in shadows and its blatant trickery out front. By age 15, I'd learned that no leader on earth could make the world safe. It was a frightening realization. For years I mourned a betrayal from a betrayer that had no face. Angst tore at my soul.

One night when I was nineteen years old, I decided to take a drive to get away from it all after a stressful week at work. I didn't know where to go. It was dark, and a heavy fog set in. I became hopelessly lost. For hours I tried desperately to find my way out of the fog, but with each turn my headlights cut circles through a thick, white blanket only to reflect another yellow dead-end sign. Terrified, I began to panic. My inner struggle, which had tortured me for years, was enacted on that road. The fog, dead-end signs, and feeling hopelessly lost became a metaphor for the fear with which I had lived for years.

Finally, on an open stretch of road, I began climbing uphill and out of the fog. My struggle had come to an end. Strangely, although it was the middle of the night, I could see clearly for a great distance. A quiet luminosity lit the mountainous landscape.

It was on that mountain road in the middle of the night that I experienced—for the first time in my adult life—pure beauty.

My Ford Mustang's engine roared with a steady hum as I climbed all the way to the peak of the pass. The increasing elevation restored my faith in life. But that was just a glimpse of the power I came in contact with that night. At the very top I pulled to the side of the road and stepped out. A night sky filled with stars cradled my shoulders, and I was forever awakened by an exquisiteness beyond words.

Driving down the mountain at dawn, I knew I had been forever changed by the stars that night. I had been given insights I could not name, and they would guide me—even if it took years—to the realization that true prosperity can only come from understanding those two all-too-human worlds. The code to prosperity is hidden in the open path.

That mountaintop decision never left me. It drove my life's work and led me to understand that we must emerge from the fog within to discover life's real opportunities. We must be open to receive what life with a capital "L" has to offer.

My journey to put into words the insights I gained in an instant of greater consciousness has taken decades and involved formal study in the social sciences and integral psychology. As one of the foremost experts on guiding others to their greatest potential, I've helped thousands of people for more than twenty years. I am considered a pioneer in the field of tapping personal energy to improve our daily lives, make us more productive, and allow us to stay on open paths to new heights.

Through my long-term practice as a licensed psychotherapist and executive consultant, as well as years of facilitating transformational programs at my institute, I have gained a powerful understanding of how to awaken this wisdom and power in you.

Mountaintop Prosperity: Move Quickly to New Heights in Life, Work and Money invites you on a journey to discover the open path in your life.

The code to prosperity is hidden in the open path.

Chapter 1
In *Consider Your Goals*, you will meet three remarkable women who have all discovered the open path to mountaintop prosperity.

Chapter 2
Avoid Mountaintop Dead Ends reveals three paths that will keep you stuck. Exploring them will help you understand, with great clarity, why the open path is the only path that will take you to new heights in your life.

Chapter 3
Breakthroughs—Eight Steps to the Mountaintop will equip you with landmarks to help you understand that, above all, your inner world holds the key to mountaintop prosperity.

Chapter 4
You will *Meet Your Great Latent Self* and learn how to bring this creative aspect of your being out of dormancy.

Chapter 5
Develop Mountaintop Thinking will teach you how to expand your mind while still being focused, tap into greater creativity, protect your big ideas, and increase your personal authority.

Chapter 6
Persist Through Challenges will help you discover what to do when you hit bumps on the open path.

Chapter 7
In *Develop a Triumphant Approach*, you will learn how to get and stay unstuck.

Chapter 8

Stoke the Fire in Your Belly will show you how to keep your passion alive, listen to your spirit, and go for what is most important.

Chapter 9

Surrender to the Highest Good equips you to understand your amphibious nature, as true prosperity requires that we float on the currents of life as well as walk on the shore. You will discover the magic of momentum and how to direct your life toward the highest good.

Chapter 10

Cultivate Your Courage to Love will take you to the animated intersection between aspirations and self-love and help you develop the crucial skill of transforming grudges into gratitude.

Chapter 11

Embrace the World highlights the significance of drawing on your collaborative nature to understand that the open path never ends.

Support for Your Climb

The *Mountaintop Prosperity Workbook* offers quotes from prior chapters along with thought provoking questions. By completing this section you will discover how to avoid dead ends, stay on the open path and journey to your mountaintop.

Mountaintop Prosperity: Move Quickly to New Heights in Life, Work and Money will teach you how to find the open path to true prosperity. You will learn that you are capable of creating the life you desire when you live from the depths of your soul.

An invitation is awaiting in the following pages to unveil the magic that is your birthright when you choose to live in the world of love rather than the world of despair. I am honored to be one of your guides along the way.

PART I

Understanding Mountaintop Prosperity

Chapter One

Consider Your Goals

Creating a truly rewarding life is not a simple step-by-step process. In fact, it is not a step-by-step process at all. All creation is complex, and you may marvel to discover that mountaintop prosperity is the most complex process you will ever experience.

To achieve mountaintop prosperity, personal desire and universal flow must meet on a surreal plane of reality that dances with the possible. A simple step-by-step process could never get you there. This doesn't mean, however, that achieving mountaintop prosperity is difficult. In fact, one of the amazing truths about mountaintop prosperity is that it isn't difficult at all.

Throughout this book, stories of three remarkable women—Rachel, Audrey, and Stella—will unfold to show that while it isn't a step-by-step process, there is a pattern to mountaintop prosperity that governs the open path. Discovering this pattern will allow you to move to new heights quickly.

. . .

"I love my life," Rachel says. "A short time ago, I was lonely and bored. I felt as though I was just going through the motions in life. I complained a lot and often got sucked into other people's complaining.

"I was twenty-five pounds heavier and hated how I felt. It was hard to move. I had just turned forty and thought my fading quality of life was all about getting older. Because of my age, I couldn't believe life had more to offer. I thought I had really blown it.

"Things have changed." Rachel—fit and trim—gestures toward herself with a twinkle in her eye. She is wearing a beautiful rose-colored silk dress and dazzling gold necklace.

"*I* have changed, and it's not just my makeover," she explains. "Today I'm happy with both who I am and the life I've created."

Rachel continues her story:

You see, I used to work as a customer service rep for an appliance company. Being on the phone all day long solving people's problems with their stoves, refrigerators, washers, and dryers was so mentally exhausting that by the end of the day I didn't want to speak to anyone. But when I discovered the open path and decided to follow it, my life changed completely.

Now I regularly travel throughout the United States as a surgical supply sales representative and consultant. I am mentally on fire, learning more every day. I have so much energy after work that I have a full social calendar. My life is so much fun!

In terms of my work, I feel proud to be part of a team of professionals dedicated to improving people's quality of life. I make more money than I ever thought possible.

I take fun vacations and have great friends. The sky is the limit.

I am now feeling more ready than ever to meet that special someone. I know that will happen, because I am on the open path, and I am willing to make my next mountaintop move for it to happen.

. . .

Stella, a thirty-eight-year-old woman, says that she had known about the open path to mountaintop prosperity since she was young. She had never questioned that it existed but didn't know it was for her. She couldn't let herself believe that she could be, in her words, "one of the amazing people in life who got to be on the open path." Her confusion stemmed from her family, who didn't believe such a path existed and discouraged Stella from getting her hopes up about creating an incredible life.

Stella's story:

While I'd always known about the open path, I didn't know that I knew. That probably sounds funny, but it is the truth. When I was young—not even 13—I would watch television with my family, and I'd zone in on the one character who prevailed because of her inner strength. I was so inspired. When the show was over, I always felt depressed, because to my family it was just a made-up story only for entertainment. For me it was about what was possible for some people. The shows were maps. And some people in real life got to take the journey. I would pray that it would be me, but I didn't trust it was possible, because I was a "nobody." I really believed the open path was for glamorous stars who had a lot of money and connections.

I think my biggest problem wasn't about trusting it was real. My biggest problem was that I had no one to talk to about it. I felt like an outsider in my own life because none of my friends or family believed in the open path, yet I was consumed by it. I had long conversations with my great latent self all the time, and I didn't even know that was what I was doing! It was as if I lived in two separate realities, and it was driving me crazy.

I finally made the decision to follow the open path, even though it was the scariest decision I ever made. I thought it meant leaving the people I loved behind. As it turned out, none of my relationships ended—I just outgrew my way of being in them. I became more authentic.

. . .

In the next story, a woman named Audrey describes that discovering the open path was a complete surprise and that it changed her life forever.

I first discovered the open path after a long period of turmoil. I was in the midst of an ugly divorce and child custody battle. My heart was torn into pieces. I did not know how on earth I could go through the divorce and keep my life intact.

My concentration had gotten so bad that I feared losing my job and becoming financially destitute. How would I care for my children and aging mother? In addition to two children at home, I was my mother's main caregiver. I worried night and day.

Then one evening—I will never forget it—I was lying in bed wailing in grief, and a sudden calm came over me. I felt a warmth I had never before experienced. It was visceral. I knew at a very deep level everything was going to be okay. I did not know how. I just knew that I did not need to fight so hard, that a path had opened and I would find my way.

Thankfully, I had amazing support in my life. A group of women who had all lived on the open path for years had been pulling me toward it. Until that night, I really didn't know what they were talking about, but their strength inspired me. They had survived similar heartbreak and shared powerful stories about finding their way to better lives by following the open path. That night I knew what they were talking about for the first time. I knew it was real.

. . .

While the path is always there, it can be truly experienced only when we have a sincere willingness to follow it.

Rachel, Stella, and Audrey are all examples of people who discovered the open path to mountaintop prosperity and chose to follow it. Their stories illustrate that regardless of how you grew up, your circumstances, or your past failures, it is never too late to step onto the open path. The stories also show that

mountaintop prosperity must come from a personal and meaningful commitment to a greater life experience. While the path
is always there, it can be truly experienced only when we have
a sincere willingness to follow it.

How Will Your Personal Story Change?

Following the open path to mountaintop prosperity will transform your personal story. Your personal story is the story you
tell yourself and others about who you are. You tell your story
all the time. Much of your personal story is shared nonverbally.
It is expressed not only in what you say but how you live.

Considering your personal story is crucial because it defines
both your potential and your self-imposed limits. Notice how
you tell your personal story to yourself and others through the
way you present yourself, what you think, how you speak, what
you say, what you are passionate about, and even what you love
and hate.

As you discover the personal story you have been telling
yourself and others, don't worry if there are parts you don't like.
These will be transformed as you step onto the open path and
begin your climb up the mountain.

In fact, it is not only *possible* to change your personal story
but *necessary* that both you and your story be transformed by
your journey toward the mountaintop.

. . .

"I had to change my personal story if I wanted mountaintop
prosperity," Audrey explains. "There was no way around it. I had
to let go of the notion that changing my personal story meant
that I was being fake. I needed to understand and really believe
that telling a new story was about offering a bigger truth about
who I am.

"I was no longer willing to be defined by two failed marriages, both of which ended after my husbands had affairs.

"I was no longer willing to see myself as a latchkey kid who fixed dinner for my mother when I was only eleven years old because I knew she would be too tired from working two jobs to fix dinner for me.

"I was no longer willing to define myself as a fatherless daughter because my dad was killed while driving drunk before I could walk.

"No, I could no longer define myself by these terrible life experiences. If I was to find the open path, I needed to believe a bigger truth about myself."

. . .

Finding the open path to the mountaintop is an authentic journey ... as you begin to climb the mountain, you will change.

We cannot achieve mountaintop prosperity through a rational plan. A rational plan—like a business plan or even traditional goal setting—will never take us to the height of our potential. We can only create mountaintop prosperity in our lives through engaging in a journey of discovery and uncovering the gifts that lie dormant in our *great latent self*. It is an emotional journey where themes of loss and overcoming hardship are common.

Climbing the mountain toward greater prosperity requires that you leave an old life behind to discover a new and better one. Leaving the old can create tremendous grief, while discovering new life fills us with elation. On the mountain path, make room for both grief and elation. Both are real, and both are part of the journey.

Finding the open path to the mountaintop is an authentic journey. Through it you will discover who you really are. As you begin to climb the mountain, you will change. If you are already halfway up the mountain or even three-quarters of the way up, you will continue to change, because every step toward greater prosperity is a transformational journey.

Celebrate your changes, the ones in yourself and in your life, because you are reinventing yourself. By celebrating, we are saying, *Yes! This is who I am now, and this is who I am becoming.*

How Will Your Views Change?

By considering how your views on life will change, you will give yourself greater permission to create mountaintop prosperity. We must let go of the old views and beliefs that limit us so that we may embrace a life of greater potential.

Your view of money and material possessions will greatly influence the degree and speed at which you attain mountaintop prosperity. An important question to ask yourself is "how do I really feel about money and material possessions?"

Is money an easy topic for you to think about, or is it a source of angst and turmoil? How do you feel about material possessions? Are they important to you? If they are important, do you feel guilty because they are? Is greater wealth good or bad in your eyes? What makes it good or bad?

Will your views serve you as you climb the mountain? Answer this question with all sincerity because your views create the lens through which you will see the world and take the next step on the open path. If your views are not aligned with your desires, you will be traveling toward a dead end.

. . .

"When I started making more money, I felt really weird," Rachel says. "I had never made more than just enough to cover my bills and go out with friends once in a while. My income literally tripled the first year of my new job, and it was, honestly, a little hard to deal with.

"I had always thought that people who drove really nice cars were full of themselves, but I found myself wanting a really nice car. I had to get used to thinking of money differently. I had to tell myself to let go of my tension about it. I had more than enough. I did not need to pinch pennies any longer."

. . .

Is it okay for you to have more than others? When you discover the open path and climb to the top of the mountain, you will accumulate more in your life than you ever thought possible.

Perhaps "more" is that car you have always wanted. Maybe more is an educational opportunity or travel to far-away places. More may mean getting involved with service projects or even philanthropy that you cannot afford now, such as offering financial support to causes you believe in or traveling to other countries to help out in times of crisis.

How Will Your Actions Change?

Along with greater resources and material possessions, mountaintop prosperity brings greater freedom and a knowing that we own our own time. How will you use your freedom and time? Will you choose to develop your talents?

. . .

"When I first committed to the open path, my new life was pretty empty," Stella explains. "While I didn't really lose anyone per se, I didn't have much in common with them anymore. In fact, I didn't have much going on at all—no hobbies or activities to look forward to. I didn't know what to do with myself until I consciously decided to develop myself. That's when things really began to change.

"I liked music, so I started taking piano lessons and attending community music events. I had to push past feeling awkward and shy about going places alone. I began setting goals for myself—things that were important to me, like walking several times a week and getting involved in the community to meet new people.

"When I joined the local theater, things really started to shift. My life became exciting. This gave me the confidence to go back to school and follow my dream of becoming a doctor."

. . .

How will you develop yourself? How will you develop your mind, heart, body, and passion? With mountaintop prosperity, every aspect of our life can be developed. Setting healthy goals from the open path allows us to live on that surreal plane of reality that dances with the possible.

Your Greatest Hopes

Hope is a sign of vitality. With it, anything is possible.

. . .

Audrey says, "At first, my greatest hope was just for my emotional pain to go away. I was in such deep grief that I couldn't get beyond it to hope for more. But as I healed, I started to understand that hoping for more had a purpose and that I needed to hope for more just to stay on the open path. The pain had lessened considerably, but it wasn't enough to just be free of pain. That was a starting point, not an end point.

Hope is a sign of vitality.
With it, anything is possible.

"In realizing that the word *hope* itself held power, I understood that it was the ticket to getting more out of life. I began to lean into hope. I hoped for things like more free time and more money to spend on my kids. And it wasn't an old feeling of just wishing, like when I used to wish my marriage would get better. No, it was a new feeling on the open path—my hope felt real. It felt powerful, and I had a much stronger belief in it. I was amazed at how often my hopes quickly became reality."

. . .

Wishing and hoping are very different things. Hope carries real personal energy, while wishing is a mere thought (often originating from an abyss of hopelessness). To stay on the open path, you must have real personal energy, the kind that hope provides us.

Mountaintop prosperity requires that we keep our hopes high. While the changes in our lives may not be immediately apparent, with hope everything changes because we have changed— our lens has changed.

Striving to have the hope of a child and the wisdom of an elder allows us to be patient and strong in our hope. Imagine a meter that registers low, medium, and high hopes. Keeping our hopes high takes us to hope portals, portals to a future where dreams can become reality.

Mountaintop prosperity requires fearlessness.

Your Greatest Fears

Are you afraid of the open path? Even though discovering the open path for the first time brings a feeling of relief and even jubilation, it is common to fear taking that initial step and beginning the mountaintop journey.

Sort through your fears. What do you fear most about mountaintop prosperity? Is it the journey or the destination? How do you typically deal with fear? Does it push you back or do you push through?

Mountaintop prosperity requires fearlessness. This doesn't mean that we don't feel fear—we may feel it very powerfully. It means that we are aware of another part of us that does not feel fear, a part of us that is fearless.

As we push past our fear, putting one foot in front of the other and taking one step at a time toward the mountaintop, we realize that it is the fearless part of us that is moving. Our fearlessness is taking each step even though another part of us may be trembling. The fearless part of us will continue to gain momentum, and our trembling will cease.

. . .

"I had a lot more fear than I even realized," says Rachel. "I believe that is why I stayed in my customer service position for so long. I had done well in college and graduated with a degree in business, but I did not have the confidence after I graduated to think of myself as a career woman. My fear stopped me from even considering that I could develop a real career. My fear made it difficult to believe that I could be successful in my career or my life."

By stepping onto the open path, Rachel experienced true victory over her fear, a victory that came from recognizing her fearlessness and choosing to allow *it* to move her forward.

. . .

Your Mountaintop Message

A natural part of traveling the open path is wanting to share it with others. As we take each step, learning about mountaintop prosperity and how to get there, mountaintop messages begin to form. We find ourselves thinking of inspiring ideas to share with others: what we've learned, how we've grown, what we've discovered. It's vital that we keep track of our mountaintop messages and watch how they change over time. Through this practice, we witness and validate our own discoveries and lay claim to our own growth.

. . .

"My mountaintop message," says Stella, "is to be yourself. Do not ever let anyone make you feel weird for knowing about the open path. There really is a mountaintop in our lives, and mountaintop prosperity is waiting for us. Being on the open path is the best feeling in the world."

. . .

"My mountaintop message is about not being a victim," says Audrey. "You are a victim when you allow your past to define you. It is just not okay. You are victimizing yourself. Once you drop that story, the world will drop it too. We all deserve to drop a personal story that limits us. It is not as hard as it might seem."

. . .

"My mountaintop message is about joy," Rachel says. "Joy is attainable. I think it comes to us when we accept our responsibility to work our way up that mountain, to know that no one can do it for us. Joy comes from finding the open path and following it."

. . .

What is your mountaintop message? Even if you haven't begun climbing the mountain, your mountaintop message is already in you and will change and evolve as you follow the open path.

Write it, shout it, sing it, dance it, or even create an art project to express it. The important thing is to express and celebrate your mountaintop message—and to witness yourself changing through it. The expression that we give to the mountaintop journey influences that journey. Our message is another way of saying, *Yes, this is who I am now that I'm on the open path.*

Imagine Your Life Improving

Think about every aspect of your life and how it will improve with mountaintop prosperity. What will your life look like in both everyday routines and profound experiences? How will mountaintop prosperity improve your relationships, your health, your work? How will it change how you spend your leisure time? How will you live your life on the open path? With mountaintop prosperity, your life can be bigger and brighter than you ever thought possible.

Chapter Two

Avoid Mountaintop Dead Ends

Once we step onto the open path, we must watch out for dead ends. Dead ends weaken us. They take time and energy away from the open path.

At first it's easy to mistake a dead end for the open path. That happens because the path we are traveling may *seem* acceptable, but it may be leading nowhere.

Dead ends are life experiences and choices that leave us feeling empty. They involve activities that hurt us, such as being in unhealthy relationships or work environments. We are heading for a dead end when we waste time or live in chaos. We are heading for a dead end when our limited beliefs keep us stuck.

First Mountaintop Dead End: Too Selfish

We are all born selfish, and being selfish ensures our survival. Have you ever met an unselfish toddler? Of course not, because they don't exist. As long as parents meet their child's needs and at the same time set healthy limits, the child will naturally grow beyond its all-consuming, selfish approach to life.

It's valuable to look at the dead end of being too selfish on the open path, and it is important to do so without shame. Letting go of all selfishness isn't possible (and we don't need to eliminate all selfish tendencies on the open path), but being *too* selfish means that you are out of control and are overly focused on yourself.

. . .

Rachel comments on her experience with the dead end of selfishness: "I have to admit that I got a bit selfish when I first found the open path. For the first time in my life, I was happy— really happy—and I just did not know when to stop. I was shopping too much, socializing too much, and burning the candle at both ends. I was starting to rack up quite a bit of debt when I realized I was heading for a dead end. I was out of control."

. . .

Life becomes very narrow when you are only focusing on getting more.

Being too selfish on the open path is a common temptation; all the hard work it takes just to climb that mountain makes it easy to justify selfish behaviors. The real problem with being too selfish is that the need can never be filled. There will never be enough money, fun, connection, or attention to fill the bottomless pit in our being when selfishness has gotten out of control.

Intense selfishness turns to greed. Life becomes very narrow when you are only focusing on getting more. Reaching the top of the mountain requires an expanded view of self and life.

Avoiding the too-selfish dead end requires that we engage in the right amount of selfishness. We can have fun accumulating material possessions and having an exciting social life while at the same time keeping a larger perspective of what the open path is all about. Getting to the top of the mountain means discovering a satisfaction in life we never thought possible.

Second Mountaintop Dead End: Too Selfless

We are too selfless when we choose to deny our own needs and desires. Do you spend your time, energy, and even money on others to the detriment of yourself? While it is wonderful to be caring and generous, being too selfless leads to anger and resentment.

Money, if you are too selfless, can even be seen as evil. These thoughts and ways of living will not allow you to reach the top of the mountain and experience true mountaintop prosperity.

. . .

"I always thought it was good to be selfless," Audrey says. "Growing up feeling responsible for my mother, it seemed strange and really wrong to consider my own needs and desires. I even thought people who had a lot of money were bad people. I didn't think it was fair that some people had to work so hard for so little while others seemed to work so little and had so much.

"To be honest, I still don't think it's fair, but once I discovered the open path, I quickly learned that being too selfless leads to a dead end. My personal needs and desires needed to be more important to me. I learned to take them more seriously. I realized that once my own needs and desires were met, I could get involved in solving some of the problems of the world that sickened me. I would be vital enough to really make a difference."

. . .

If you are too selfless, you will be forever unfulfilled. You will live in angst and fear that you are wasting your life. Yet having some degree of selflessness is important. As you travel up the mountain on the open path, there will be many opportunities to serve others.

Third Mountaintop Dead End: Too Self-Caring

If you have a belief that you must protect yourself at all times, you are too self-caring to reach the mountaintop. Being too self-caring comes from adopting a victim mentality and feeling as though you cannot let your guard down.

While good self-care is important for everyone, being *too* self-caring blocks a vital flow in life. Being too self-caring keeps your life small. It traps you in sadness. Your heart is not open to others, and you certainly won't get your intimacy needs met.

. . .

"I did not think it was possible to be too self-caring," Stella remarks. "Years before I discovered the open path, I read a book about self-care. It became my bible, especially when I felt most alone. I became so self-caring that there was no room to receive all of what life has to offer. When I first stepped onto the open path, my hyper-focus on self-care was preventing me from receiving the pleasant surprises in life. I was quickly heading for a dead end."

. . .

We need to make room on the open path for pleasant surprises, for getting our needs met by life in ways we never imagined. While being too self-caring will take us to a dead end, it is important to have the right amount of self-care. When we engage in the right amount of self-care, we are preparing for mountaintop prosperity. We are getting ourselves ready for the best that life has to offer.

We need to make room on the open path for
pleasant surprises, for getting our needs met by life
in ways we never imagined.

Frustration

If you are feeling frustrated in your life, you are heading for a dead end. Frustration is a landmark telling you that you are not on the open path. Even if you think your frustration is caused by not being able to achieve mountaintop goals, the truth is that frustration may be preventing you from those goals.

Frustration will drain your personal life energy and lead you to defeat.

Isolation

Isolation is another sign that you are heading for a dead end. You have left the open path and have withdrawn from a full life. This creates carelessness and reduces feelings of self-worth.

It is common for people on the open path to feel isolated simply because they are leaving behind a life they have always known. But regardless of where you are on the journey, do not isolate yourself. Instead, stay engaged with life to avoid this common dead end.

Isolation prevents personal energy from being shared, which in turn prevents universal flow from moving through your life.

Powerlessness

Powerlessness is another sign that you are heading for a dead end. A sense of powerlessness will create feelings of weakness, helplessness, and hopelessness within you. It will lower your self-esteem. One of the most salient features of the open path is an experience of empowerment.

Powerlessness will prevent your personal energy from building.

Jealousy

Perhaps the strongest emotional landmark warning that you are heading for a dead end is jealousy. Jealousy is a very toxic emotion; it tells you that you have taken a wrong turn either within yourself or in your life.

Whether you envy others' advantages or achievements or you

compare yourself to others and come up short, you are heading for a dead end.

If you are projecting your own talents onto others and thinking they are better at something in which you want to excel, you are heading for a dead end.

If you are jealous of others because you want what they have, you are heading for a dead end.

Wanting to be at the top of the mountain but being blocked by jealousy creates a toxicity in you and in your relationships. Jealousy lowers your self-concept. When your personal energy becomes toxic, you will lose the vitality you need to stay on the open path.

The answer to all dead ends is breaking through to the open path. Understanding how to break through is the key to reaching mountaintop prosperity.

Chapter Three

Breakthroughs—Eight Steps to the Mountaintop

The open path to the mountaintop is easily recognized by your own personal energy. There is vitality on the open path, an excitement, a flow.

First Breakthrough: Finding the Open Path

When we are on the open path, we have discovered our great latent self. This is the deepest part of us, which holds the key to the most powerful, loving, and successful aspects of our being.

Great means surpassing even your highest expectations. *Latent* means resting in potential. Your *great latent self* is the part of you that, while resting in potential, holds a version of yourself that surpasses your highest hopes.

Your great latent self has always, from the beginning of your life, rested in your being in potential. Finding the open path wakes up your great latent self and brings it out of dormancy.

If you ever find yourself on a dead end, simply reconnect with your great latent self by stepping back onto the open path.

Traveling the open path in your life allows for selfishness, self-lessness, and self-caring all to be present in the right degree. The open path is not about being perfect. It is about being authentic. It is not about following someone else's way of life or about commandments regarding how to live. It is about finding your own commandments, knowing that because they rise from your great latent self, they will be good, true, and powerful.

> *The open path is not about being perfect.*
> *It is about being authentic.*

The strong desire to access our great latent self is universal; it is inherent in all people. Knowing *how* to access our great latent self, however, is much more mysterious. It can seem to be locked in a code relatively few people understand. Finding the open path unlocks the code.

Once we are on the open path, the patterns of our own life and potential are revealed. How to reach mountaintop prosperity becomes more obvious.

. . .

Rachel says that for her, traveling the open path was tentative at first. "I second guessed the open path countless times before I started taking it seriously. Out of nowhere, I had experiences, for lack of a better word, that would completely shift my thinking.

"Flashes of a better life would come to me. I could even see myself in a different job and living in a different home. I shrugged them off, telling myself they were just little day-dreams. The day I realized that the flashes were real and they were guiding me is the day my life became mine."

. . .

Finding and traveling the open path significantly increases personal energy. It frees up our great latent self so that we may live lives beyond our highest expectations.

Second Breakthrough: Mountaintop Insight

Stepping onto the open path comes with a glimpse of a power beyond what we had previously known in our adult life. This power may be described as an unseen flow in the universe. Mountaintop insight, the second breakthrough on the open path, activates a curiosity about this power and makes us realize we have lived a life void of true eagerness before discovering the open path.

On the open path, curiosity about this power becomes part of our life experience. We realize that it is our great latent self that is curious. Like an old friend, our curiosity has returned to our lives. When it does return, we may remember times as a child when we were naturally curious. But this time our curiosity is different. Whereas our child self was curious about what we saw, tasted, smelled, heard, and touched in the world, our curiosity is now about what we cannot see, taste, smell, hear, or touch. Our curiosity is about universal flow.

When we break through to mountaintop insight, our visual perception often shifts. Colors look brighter. The universe appears to be animated like never before.

. . .

"The calm I felt that night when I was wailing in grief was my first mountaintop insight," says Audrey. "It was a powerful experience that stopped my tears from flowing. I strived to listen to that calm as though I was tipping my ear to the side, even though there was no sound in the room.

"It was an inner sound wave. I do not know how else to describe it. It moved through my heart, and my grief changed in that moment. My pain was no longer that of loss. It suddenly became the pain of birth. My new life was birthing."

. . .

When we break through to mountaintop insight, we find ourselves witnessing our lives while we are living them. We watch ourselves learn, grow, and develop.

Third Breakthrough: Mountaintop Inspiration

With mountaintop inspiration, we experience a rising of the great latent self, the part of us that has remained dormant until now, and this brings us great passion. With the rising of the great latent self, we have an expanded sense of the possible. We become aware of synergism, an energy that we can only experience when our great latent self is coming out of dormancy and living life.

. . .

"When I decided to follow the open path, I signed up for school," says Stella. "It is what I always wanted to do, but it was a terrifying experience. I was the first girl in my family to go to college. My brother went to college on the GI bill, but the girls in the family did not have that opportunity. We were supposed to just get married and have kids.

"Once I stepped onto the open path, I was so inspired. It did not even seem like a choice. My friends at the theater encouraged me to sign up for just one class. I loved it. It was so energizing. I kept going, and the time went by so quickly that, before I knew it, I was applying for medical school. My secret dream to become a doctor was within reach.

"Being on the open path made everything possible. My passion carried me all the way through medical school and my residency. Becoming a doctor was the best decision I ever made."

. . .

The third breakthrough to mountaintop inspiration brings a greater sense of well-being. The rising of our great latent self is a strengthening experience. We feel capable and inspired to take the next steps on the open path, and we begin to quickly gain more prosperity in all areas of our life.

Fourth Breakthrough: Mountaintop Recognition

We have made the fourth breakthrough to mountaintop recognition when we begin to trust our greater insights. A multidimensional experience of life opens. With mountaintop recognition there is an undeniable awareness of a nonlinear reality.

*The rising of our great latent self
is a strengthening experience.*

We understand that life is much more mysterious than we had previously thought and that while we are living in the world of ordinary affairs, something extraordinary is happening in our lives.

We have a greater appreciation for the interconnectedness of all things, not only in the ecosphere of the natural world but in the interconnectedness of all people, all thoughts, all breaths, and all desires that come from our great latent selves. At some level of consciousness, we recognize that our personal desire and universal flow have met on the surreal plane of reality that dances with the possible.

. . .

"For me, my intuitive understanding of all things was a surprise," says Rachel. "All of a sudden, I just got it. I knew how to be happy. Once I decided to leave my old job and pursue my dreams, I intuitively understood how to get there. I really fell in love with life, and I am still in love with life.

"I tell everyone about mountaintop prosperity and the open

path. I want everyone to know what I know. It is really incredible. It is hard to contain. I have to be careful not to be too happy around some people. Not everyone is interested in mountaintop prosperity. They just cannot allow themselves to believe it really exists, but I do. I recognize it."

. . .

Rachel had a glimpse of her own power as well as the power in the universe. She was connecting the two and playing with the possibilities of that connection. Once we recognize this connection power, our understanding of life is changed forever. There is no way to go back. Luckily, we would not want to put our great latent self back to sleep even if we could.

Fifth Breakthrough: Carrying the Mountaintop Flame
With the fifth breakthrough, we are carrying the mountaintop flame and have fallen in love with life. We have a heightened appreciation for beauty and a desire to tell everyone about how incredible life is. We want to wake up early and stay up late so we don't miss any of the beauty of life.

When we carry the mountaintop flame, we trade a static life for a commitment to the possible. We feel as though we are walking with the power of a thousand generations. We realize that our definition of mountaintop prosperity reaches beyond a desire for material success alone and includes engaging in matters of worldly importance. We have an urgency and potency of will to make a difference in the world.

We realize through the fifth breakthrough that we can have both material success and a significant and meaningful life. We are carrying the flame for both.

Sixth Breakthrough: Mountaintop Resonance
The sixth breakthrough, mountaintop resonance, allows us to tap into the *sphere of genius*. The sphere of genius is the higher intelligence of the universe that we have come to know on

the open path as universal flow. The sixth breakthrough taps us directly into the sphere of genius, and our clarity about life is astonishing.

With the sixth breakthrough we acquire mountaintop sonar. We feel and sense our next moves toward mountaintop prosperity.

The moment we experience the sixth breakthrough and tap in directly to the sphere of genius, we desire to tap in as much as possible. We recognize when we are—and are not—tapped in, and we begin to adjust our lifestyle so that we may tap in more often.

With the sixth breakthrough, we develop a mountaintop practice to live more consciously on every level.

Adjusting our lifestyle means changing the way we live because we realize that there is a correlation between how we live and how well we resonate with the sphere of genius. We begin to consider our diets, our health regimens, our sleep, and our creative pursuits as all-important in terms of building our capacity to resonate with the sphere of genius.

With the sixth breakthrough, we develop a mountaintop practice to live more consciously on every level. Perhaps our mountaintop practice involves regular prayer or meditation. Perhaps we engage in a physical exercise practice such as yoga or running.

With the sixth breakthrough to mountaintop resonance, our practice is in the service of bringing our great latent self out of dormancy and into our lives. When this has been accomplished, our mountaintop sonar develops and we resonate with the sphere of genius for longer periods of time.

. . .

"To increase my mountaintop sonar, I kept going back to that life-changing calm," Stella explains. "I would meditate on the feeling that changed my life forever, and one day I realized I was tapping into the sphere of genius. It is a dimension that has all the answers. I had to teach myself how to resonate with that calm to tap back into it over and over again. I was compelled to connect with the sphere of genius as often as I could."

. . .

Seventh Breakthrough: Mountaintop Streaming

The seventh breakthrough, mountaintop streaming, allows us to tap into the sphere of genius at will. We begin to stream the higher intelligence of the universe through our own minds and bodies. Through mountaintop streaming, we learn to articulate extraordinary intelligence.

At work, we offer solutions that are out of the box. At home, our creativity streams endlessly. With mountaintop streaming, we optimize our use of time. We always seem to know the next step without even considering it. We become loyal to a higher and clearer understanding of all things and even say things that are so profound we surprise ourselves and others.

. . .

With mountaintop streaming, we optimize our use of time.

"At times, I can tap into the sphere of genius at will," says Rachel. "It is amazing. I feel like I am streaming the most incredible information. I am not even sure where it comes from. All of a sudden, I just have the answer—the solution to a problem at work or a way to take that trip I have always wanted to take.

"One time my boss asked me where I wanted to see myself in the organization. I said without even thinking, 'I want two things: to be where I am most needed and to be where I am most happy, and I know they are not separate positions. How could they be?' That is when we realized I should be in my current position.

"When I am able to tap into the sphere of genius, I am most happy, but I can't always tap in on cue. Most of the time, I just hold the intention and then, within hours or days, I find myself tapped in. It is not immediate all the time."

. . .

For Stella, connecting to the sphere of genius is more constant.

"Perhaps because I felt it when I watched those television shows when I was young, I can tap into the sphere of genius at will. It has always been there. I know how to access it. My challenge used to be streaming it without reservation. I was afraid it would separate me from others. It did not—my life is incredibly full."

. . .

"I can tap into the sphere of genius and stream it at will when I am alone and in a quiet space," Audrey says, "but I cannot yet stream when I am around people. So I consciously tap into the sphere of genius every morning and every evening, and the streaming I get from that carries me through the day."

Eighth Breakthrough: Mountaintop Identification

The eighth breakthrough: mountaintop identification, takes us to the top of the mountain. At the top of the mountain we realize at a very deep level that the sphere of genius is an aspect of ourselves. It is our birthright. Through the open path, our great latent self has risen out of dormancy, and the sphere of genius has moved into our constant awareness. We now live on that surreal plane of reality where personal desire and universal flow dance with the possible.

Through the eighth breakthrough, we realize that everything *is* possible—including the life, work, and money we desire. The urgency to get to the top of the mountain has settled because we recognize that we *are* at the top of the mountain. A quiet self-confidence builds.

Through mountaintop identification, we effortlessly utilize our highest potential in all aspects of our lives. We have complete trust in ourselves and the universe.

Mountaintop identification is a muscle that must be developed. At times, we are there strongly, and the next day we may feel like we are at the bottom of the mountain again, needing to climb our way back up.

> *Through mountaintop identification,*
> *we effortlessly utilize our highest potential*
> *in all aspects of our lives.*

When we have touched the top of the mountain at least once in our lives and have recognize that the sphere of genius is within us and is our birthright, we can always find our way back again if we are committed to building the muscle through our commitment and life practices. We will develop faith through mountaintop identification that we are moving in the right direction even when the muscle is fatigued.

. . .

"I have been to the top of the mountain," Audrey says. "It is incredible. I know it is real even though my immediate awareness of it comes and goes. At times I know beyond a shadow of a doubt that the sphere of genius is in me, but then that truth evades me and I am back to thinking it is bigger than me.

"When I remember that I am *that* big, *that* great, *that* amazing, life is instantly *that* big, *that* great, *that* amazing. It is not just because I am thinking it so—it really is so. Things shift and move, and amazing things happen. Every aspect of my life has changed through the eighth breakthrough."

. . .

"I really know that the sphere of genius is in us. It really is true," says Stella. "I believe when more people understand this truth, the world will be a very different place. Through the sphere of genius, we will learn to live together in harmony."

PART II

Emerging Above the Fog

Chapter Four

Meet Your Great Latent Self

Your ego creates needless fear in your life, the kind of fear that—unless you understand it—will keep you from traveling the open path. The code of the ego and how it rules us was formed early in our life. It directs most of us from a place below consciousness. While we don't hear the words *be fearful*, we feel the effects of our ego's limiting direction every day of our lives.

To bring your great latent self out of dormancy, you must understand how your ego is blocking you. In fact, your ego's job is to block your great latent self. While it appears to be an unfortunate and damaging setup in the psyche, the role of the ego is actually brilliant by universal design.

Our great latent self holds such remarkable power that without a commitment to use our power for mountaintop prosperity, our ego will block it. You see, the ego strives to protect us from misusing our power. It also protects our great latent self from the harsh impact of a dead-end life.

Think of it this way: when you were too young to know

better, someone stopped you from running impulsively into the street or putting your hand on a hot burner. Someone loved you enough to keep you from hurting yourself.

The ego was encoded with the word *no*. Your ego's code—especially if it was created harshly or sloppily through trauma or abuse—will also stop you from living fully. It will prevent you from dancing fully, singing fully, or experiencing life fully, because you were taught to keep yourself back from life. You were taught that life is dangerous.

While our ego developed to protect us from the harsh realities of the world, it also keeps our great latent self in dormancy. With our great latent self blocked, the ego becomes a false personality formed out of fear rather than an authentic expression of the plane of reality that dances with the possible.

> *When you meet your great latent self,*
> *you will feel at home.*

While the ego loves to appear flashier and better than others to survive the harsh realities of the world, it takes us into an inner war. Our scars present themselves as shame, self-doubt, perfectionism, addiction, and even entitlement.

We become imprisoned when our ego rules us, and it is a prison that can be escaped only by the great latent self. Only the great latent self can climb the open path to mountaintop prosperity.

Here is the brilliance of the universal design. We must allow our great latent self to rise out of dormancy by stepping onto the open path. We must say yes to real transformation. Otherwise, we are just playing a game of attempting to reach the mountaintop through dead-end paths. Following the open path gives our great latent self permission to rise.

When you meet your great latent self, you will feel at home. You do not need to compete with others or be flashy or call attention to yourself in inauthentic ways, because your great latent self will protect you and show you how to truly meet your needs. You will grow into this deeper truth. You will experience a joy of remembering. Your needless fears will vanish.

Identify False Limits

False limits are the notions you believe about yourself without even trying. False limits keep your great latent self dormant. As Rachel described, she didn't believe she was a career woman until she let go of that false limit and discovered true success.

On the open path, your great latent self may hear your ego chatter nonsense but will not give into it. It sees your false limits for what they are: false. You must support your great latent self by choosing to let go of your ego and false limits.

. . .

Stella talks about her false limits: "I really thought I would be all alone in my life if I followed the open path, not only in terms of friends, but I didn't think it was possible to meet a man who really understood me. And then I met my husband at the theater.

"He was the funniest person I had ever known, and I really felt understood by him. He has always been encouraging. At times it was tough trying to maintain our relationship with all the demands of medical school, but we made it. I simply adore him."

. . .

"My false limit was thinking I had to settle for a boring life," says Rachel. "I was bored out of my mind in my past job. I was limiting myself by believing that I could not have more."

. . .

"It is hard to believe that my entire life was built around false limits," says Audrey. "How I approached being a caretaker made me take on the identity of someone who had no life of her own.

"As a parent, I gave all I could to my kids and lost myself in the process. I did the same thing in my marriages and had to really come to terms with the fact that my false limits—believing that my life wasn't important—contributed to my husband's affairs. I am not saying I was to blame. I am just saying I can see how it happened."

. . .

Identifying our false limits and choosing to move beyond them puts us in the ring to fight for our authentic lives, the lives we want at the mountaintop. It will take everything we have to break free from the ego's cunning, baffling, and powerful hold. The ego does not want us to journey up the mountain. It will forever believe that the mountain is the busy street that our impulsive two-year-old is heading toward.

We must allow our great latent self to speak the truth: stepping onto the open path is why we are here. It is the real journey of life that we have been awaiting. We are no longer toddlers. We are capable of keeping ourselves safe while traveling on the open path.

Traveling on the open path is a journey to the life we've always wanted—the resources, the time, the creativity, and the capacity to make a difference in the world.

Unify Your Words and Actions

Let your great latent self have the floor and discover a new inner language. When your great latent self speaks, you will hear words of encouragement, creativity, and strength. With the power of a thousand generations, your great latent self will communicate with you day and night.

Listen to your great latent self, recognize its voice, understand its intentions, and begin to unify your actions with the voice of your great latent self. This is what Stella did when she decided to go back to school to become a doctor.

While her ego was setting false limits and telling her it was not a good idea, her great latent self encouraged her to move forward, to go ahead and take just one class. As Stella listened and followed her great latent self, she became aware that this inner voice carried great wisdom.

When you begin to unify your actions with your great latent self, life becomes very simple. It is a matter of following that inner voice, even though the ego will push back every step of the way. By following your great latent self, you will discover that through your actions, you are creating your mountaintop life.

*Traveling on the open path is a journey to
the life we've always wanted.*

Discover Your Self-Authority

Self-authority means that above all else, you trust the power and wisdom of your great latent self, knowing that when you do, you have access to the sphere of genius and are on your way to mountaintop prosperity.

With self-authority, your answers come from within. While it is a good idea, especially at first, to reach out for validation from others on the open path, you realize that validation and approval are two very different things.

Validation is about knowing that the ego can trick you into taking a dead-end path. It is about reaching out for support and guidance when you are unsure.

Approval, on the other hand, is about making yourself small and seeking permission. Approval seeking will forever keep you in the fog.

Once you discover your self-authority, let your great latent self triumph within you. Make room within yourself for your great latent self to be fully present and witness how it literally changes the way you move. Your self-authority will change how you carry your body and how you express yourself.

You have probably noticed children who carry a sense of freedom. They are not shut down. They are safe because their limits have been defined. They cannot run into the street. There is a fence for protection, but within the yard they have plenty of space to run.

Big gestures. Big smiles. Big laughter. Big animation of spirit. This is what we recover on the open path. Our self-authority allows us to live big because we have defined safe limits for ourselves. We can allow our great latent self to triumph within us because we are giving ourselves permission to be full from the inside out.

Your self-authority will change how you carry your body and how you express yourself.

Our self-authority is a capacity that, like a muscle, must be developed. You will be tested. Children who find themselves in a big, open field will be unsure if they can run freely. They will be tested by their own fear of open space. Because they have never seen a field so large, they will be uncertain about their safety.

We can be free by understanding that our great latent self, although very childlike, is our fully formed, mature self waiting to rise out of dormancy. Our great latent self is our loving adult, our inner adult who will be right there with us on the open path watching for potential danger. Our ego can be freed.

Once you find your self-authority, never relinquish it again. If you do, you will push your great latent self back into dormancy and invite your ego to rule once more.

Distinguish Your Great Latent Self
Finding the open path is a personal experience. It is yours alone, and while your open path is a sovereign domain, it will not disconnect you from life. In fact, you will be more engaged

than ever. You will discover that your great latent self is both connected to the world fully and, at the same time, very distinct and individual.

Do you remember being told when you were young that you are a unique creation, that there will never be another person on the planet quite like you, that you have a distinct fingerprint?

It is true. Your great latent self carries a distinct blueprint of your greatest potential, while your ego is formed from a standard mold. An egoic way of being in the world is quite common, while your great latent self is distinct.

Your distinctness is your greatest gift. As you travel the open path, you will develop your distinctness and this development holds your greatest potential to reach the mountaintop.

As you can see, Stella, Audrey, and Rachel are all distinct individuals on their own personal paths to the mountaintop. Each has found the open path that is right for her. Attempting to take another's path would lead to a dead end. On their distinct open paths, they will not look like one another, act like one another, dress like one another, or create a life like another. They will all create a life that is right for them.

The open path highlights our uniqueness. In the case of Audrey, Rachel, and Stella, you can appreciate how unique they all are.

A certain harmonic governs the open path. Although it is difficult to comprehend, it can be described as a unity composed of individual distinctness. Once we recognize that harmony is part of the pattern of the open path, we are free to claim our distinctness. We understand that we have an important note to play in the larger choir. We become supportive of ourselves. We grow self-respect. We show self-respect. We become dignified in our distinctness.

By bringing our great latent self out of dormancy, we will receive true appreciation and respect from others. We will be seen and met by others on the open path. We will learn more each day about the harmonic pattern and how to live as part of it.

A "Round-Up" Practice

Your great latent self naturally rounds up. What this means is that while the ego's impulse will be to shut you down, keep you small, and limit you, your great latent self will naturally round up by stretching more into life.

We may smile a bit longer or maintain eye contact meaningfully longer than we would have. Our great latent self will lean 110% toward life by contributing more, receiving more, enjoying more, experiencing more, connecting more, and finding that "more" is effortless.

The open path brings about a pleasant way of being in the world. We can tune into and use a round-up practice as a barometer to know how present our great latent self is at all times.

Are you feeling generous with your smile, with your comments, with your love? This will tell you how present your great latent self is. A round-up practice is about becoming conscious of a rounding up in our lives and leaning into the practice. Train yourself to naturally bring greater kindness, respect, admiration, and joy to yourself and others.

The real beauty of your round-up practice—and the brilliance of the universe—is that it will strengthen the muscle you need to keep your ego at bay and your great latent self present in your life.

Chapter Five

Develop Mountaintop Thinking

When the ego directs your life, you may appear strong in a blustery sense, but in reality you are weak. Ego is shallow; it doesn't root to anything other than fear.

Imagine a child stepping up for a race among friends. He is so sure of himself. He believes he will win the race because he *wants* to win. Ego tells him that he is entitled to win the race even though he is unprepared in physical strength, stamina, and speed. When he loses the race, he is angry and confused. He doesn't understand why he lost.

While the ego is rooted in fear, self is rooted to the sphere of genius and universal flow. These roots encourage our great latent self to walk, run, and race through life with the power of a thousand generations.

On the open path, the second breakthrough to mountaintop insight takes us to the understanding that while the outer world may get bumpy from time to time, our inner world needn't be. Confusion and entitlement both come from the ego. They are cues that we are out of touch with our great latent self.

. . .

Before she experienced a life-changing calm, Audrey was confused. She didn't understand why her life was miserable when she was such a good, giving, and dedicated person. Why did her husband have an affair when Audrey gave him everything she possibly could? Wasn't she entitled to more? Why did her children not give back the same degree of love and consideration she gave to them?

Audrey was in a state of confusion that led to despair. The moment she discovered the open path, however, her confusion vanished. The questions that had tortured her a moment before were no longer relevant. Through the open path, Audrey discovered mountaintop thinking.

. . .

Living with confusion will quickly take you to a dead end. That confusion will vanish immediately when you bring your great latent self out of dormancy. One way to do this is by having long conversations with your great latent self even though it may be at war with your ego at the time. While the ego may slam you with self-doubt, self-shaming, and self-criticism, you will help your great latent self break free from your ego's hold by giving it a voice. Let your great latent self take you beyond confusion.

When we demonstrate that we can get up when we fall, we allow our great latent self to prepare for the journey up the mountain. We are developing the strength, stamina, and speed we will need to reach the top.

Balance Your Thoughts

The mind is complex, and without discipline it can become our worst nightmare. The fourth breakthrough to mountaintop recognition will make it clear that your great latent self thinks differently than the ego. While your ego thinks limiting thoughts, your great latent self thinks expansively.

Expansive thoughts arise from balanced thinking in which your positive and critical thoughts work together on the open path. For instance, if you desire to go back to school and the ego tries to stop you from taking your desire seriously, it will do so by sending limiting thoughts through your mind. Your ego will tell you that going back to school is impossible, that you don't have the time, money, energy, or freedom to pursue your dream. Your critical thoughts will close your hope portal, and your positive thoughts will be nonexistent.

You may think the answer to the ego's negativity lies in developing positive thinking. Getting to the mountaintop, however, requires a more complex approach. Positive thinking alone will not keep us on the open path, but *balanced* thinking will.

Rather than merely increasing our positive thoughts or trying to eliminate our critical thoughts altogether, we must balance our thinking. As it turns out, our great latent self thrives on critical thoughts but not in the old sense of the word.

The great latent self is a wise connoisseur of life and thus aspires to be critical in the best sense of the word: critical in support of greatness.

Let your great latent self take you
beyond confusion.

Your great latent self thrives on utilizing both your positive *and* critical thoughts. Balanced thinking will support you in living on that surreal plane of reality that dances with the possible.

Your great latent self will use both your positive and critical thoughts to arrive at real, workable solutions. It may say, "It's a great idea to go back to school; going back to school will take you closer to mountaintop prosperity. You will develop yourself through going back to school. Even though it will be difficult, you will find the resources you need. School will be a great investment."

Your great latent self might also say, "In order to go back to school, you will need to work at least part time. You may feel tired at times, and it may be difficult, but you can do it." This is one of many examples of the voice of balanced thinking spoken through your great latent self.

With balanced thinking, your critical thoughts support you. They tell you what is reasonable and not reasonable for your vision.

The ego can be tricky. It can deceive you into believing that you can do anything and may even try to impersonate your great latent self. Your ego may say, "Yes, go back to school" and "Sure, it's fine to go back to school in another country. Don't worry about how it will work; it will work out! Just buy the ticket!"

There is not enough critical thinking in that approach. Ego will set you up to fail so you will have to come back to your small life and be protected from that big, dangerous world out there.

To stay on the open path, we must continually develop our self-confidence.

Your great latent self uses balanced thinking so that you will be successful. Your positive and critical thoughts will work together to support you.

Having conversations with your great latent self naturally disciplines your thoughts. Your great latent self will always defer to the sphere of genius by connecting to the higher intelligence in the universe to keep your life in balance. Turn up the volume on this great thinking and learn from it. Before long, you will be able to tap into it at will.

Develop Self-Confidence

Every day the world chips away at our self-confidence. Like a muscle, it weakens when it is not put to good use. To stay on the open path, we must continually develop our self-confidence. We must strive to make it stronger.

As we develop our self-confidence, we discover that it comes from a deep certainty. The only way to get that deep certainty is by connecting with our great latent self and the sphere of genius.

Self-confidence resonates with prosperity, and, of course, prosperity resonates with the top of the mountain.

As Audrey explains, we must affirm self-confidence on a daily basis to stay on the open path.

. . .

"Once I found the open path, I was really shaky. I had the experience of the calm that changed my life, but it was in the evening when I was alone. When I tried to carry that calm into the world, at first I failed. I became very nervous. I felt invisible to others. I could not even get the attention of my coworkers if I had a question.

"My self-confidence was very low, but through my dedication to the open path I gained greater insights about mountaintop prosperity, and this allowed me to build my self-confidence. My self-confidence was no longer hindered by what my life was reflecting to me but supported by what I was reflecting to others from my great latent self and the sphere of genius.

"I developed my self-confidence from the inside out, and before long it started being reflected back to me from the world. While I didn't think anything had changed, people began treating me with greater respect. I realized this was because I had changed. I was no longer living from the outside in but from the inside out."

. . .

When we develop self-confidence from our great latent self and the sphere of genius, our self-confidence is a shield. It becomes a buffer that keeps us from getting pulled into chaos and turmoil in the world. Carry a deep certainty about your great latent self and the sphere of genius as you live your life in the world, and watch how your interactions improve without you uttering a single word.

Most worry is needless. It comes from unbalanced thinking, lack of self-confidence, and confusion.

Chase Worry Away

Mountaintop thinking teaches us how to chase worry away. Audrey explains how this aspect of her life changed dramatically.

. . .

"If I hadn't learned how to chase worry away," she says, "my life never would have improved. I was the biggest worrier on the planet. When I realized that my great latent self never worries about anything, I began to rely more and more on *that* part of my being and realized it is possible to chase my worries away. My great latent self loves to chase worries away."

. . .

Most worry is needless. It comes from unbalanced thinking, lack of self-confidence, and confusion. With mountaintop thinking, we cease to worry. If worry is present in our lives, we can be sure we have disconnected from our great latent self. It is a sign that we have lost touch with the sphere of genius.

Still, it can be helpful to keep an eye on worry. Worry helps us understand where we are on the open path. You will probably notice that worry increases when the outer world feels overwhelming and when your shield of confidence has weakened.

Your great latent self witnesses every thought, every action, and every idea that you experience. It uses worry as a cue. If you are worrying, have a conversation with your great latent self and listen for a resolution to your problem that you can hold close to your heart.

Start that conversation early. If you allow needless worry to build, your ego will use it as fuel. By starting the conversation early and seeking resolution, you help your great latent self grow stronger and weaken ego's hold.

Strive to Stream

With mountaintop prosperity, life is never static. It is a flow. Mountaintop streaming is the ultimate use of your mind. The seventh breakthrough on the open path—mountaintop streaming—allows you to articulate in words the universal intelligence coming directly from the sphere of genius. With streaming you will naturally have great thoughts. Through mountaintop streaming, you will be guided every step of the way to the mountaintop.

Many people on the open path use a personal streaming practice. At first they set aside time to consciously stream the sphere of genius through their balanced minds. They may see themselves on the mountaintop tapping into the sphere of genius. They practice articulating what they sense, feel, hear, or know that is coming from that realm of higher intelligence.

At some point, streaming extends beyond a practice. Streaming becomes a way of life—the new normal. If you take your practice time seriously, streaming will become a habit. You will begin to stream on a more consistent basis and notice how streaming reinforces your confidence.

Nurture Your Big Ideas

Streaming brings big ideas to us, and big ideas bring about incredible passion, lighting the fire in your belly. Once you have crossed the streaming threshold, earlier breakthroughs such as mountaintop inspiration take on new meaning. We discover that the breakthroughs along the open path endlessly loop. Each time we travel them on a higher level, we do so with greater sensitivity and knowledge.

Your big ideas on the open path hold powerful seeds to greater prosperity. Nurture them. Bring them into a conversation with your great latent self and watch them grow. Do not let go of them easily—hold on to them. Ask how your ideas can become reality. Use mountaintop thinking and your balanced thoughts to consider steps to birth your big ideas. Help them grow.

Our big ideas lead to big accomplishments, and our big accomplishments lead to greater prosperity.

By getting beyond confusion, using balanced thinking, developing our self-confidence, and chasing worry away, mountaintop streaming becomes the new normal. Our big ideas lead to big accomplishments, and our big accomplishments lead to greater prosperity. When we nurture our big ideas, we take steps to help them grow.

Our great latent self is filled with more big ideas than we will ever birth in our lifetime. We can, however, nurture the most powerful of them as we follow the open path to the mountaintop. With our big ideas, we are on our way to greater prosperity and all that we hope it will be.

Chapter Six

Persist Through Challenges

The open path will naturally get bumpy from time to time. It is even possible that the sphere of genius is at play in times of challenge. Your great latent self may be taking you to the edge and asking you to push beyond to show your ego that you rule.

When we demonstrate that we will get up when we fall, our great latent self has greater room to develop us into the strong being we need to be to reach the mountaintop.

While the ego may appear strong, its strength is shallow. It's like the child who feels sure he can win the race because he *wants* to win without putting the time and energy into training. Our egos may tell us how great we are, but when put to the test, we do not have the stamina to climb the mountain.

Our great latent self is much deeper. To allow it to be fully present, we need to train, and train hard.

When you hit a bump on the open path, you must first rest for a moment. Review how that bump occurred and then stream your response to the bumpy path. The bumps in life may be like braille guiding you away from danger and making sure that you remain true to the path.

. . .

"When I first decided to move beyond being a customer service rep," Rachel says, "my life got very bumpy. I thought I could just go into my first interview with all of my customer service experience and my degree in business.

"I felt so inspired being on the open path that I thought I would get the first job I applied for. This was not the case. In fact, it took me over a year to transition. I became really discouraged at one point, but I listened to the sphere of genius and started brushing up on my sales knowledge and even took a class in medical terminology.

"It was a much harder transition than I had imagined, but I am so glad that I stayed on the open path. If I had stepped off, I would not have the life I now have."

. . .

If Rachel had used ego to charm her way into her position as a surgical sales rep and consultant, she would not be on the open path today. Her experience would have been much different. She would have felt intimidated that she did not know enough, faking her way through meetings rather than contributing at her current high level through the open path.

When the open path becomes bumpy,
increase your level of organization.

Rachel took the extra time to prepare herself and to strengthen her ability to bring her great latent self into her life in ever-increasing increments. She was persistent and recognized that the bumps on the open path were revealing her weaknesses and pointing out where she needed to be stronger to reach her mountaintop goals.

Find Your Footing in Organization

Increasing the stakes in your life by changing a career, investing in a business, joining a partnership, or simply taking your life to the next level requires solid footing on the open path.

Your footing on the open path is determined by how organized you are. When the open path becomes bumpy, increase your level of organization. This requires organizing every aspect of your life and finding the strength and clarity that being organized brings.

The open path requires that we prioritize and toss, clarifying what matters most and tossing whatever doesn't matter.

We simply cannot carry a heavy life to the mountaintop. Clutter closes the open path; it weighs us down and makes it difficult for us to climb to the top of the mountain. We need to trim on every level: our possessions, our communications, our relationships, our paperwork. A trim and streamlined life is a life that has no limit.

Our great latent self is a masterful organizer. When we understand that the higher the stakes the more important our footing, we begin to prioritize and trim our life instinctually. We will be amazed at how we intuitively prepare for our future even though we are not sure what is around the corner. When our personal desire and universal flow meet on that surreal plane of reality that dances with the possible, we realize that we were somehow prepared to reach our destination. Our lives unfold on a higher order.

Meet Challenge with Calm

"The most challenging part of my early journey," Stella recalls, "was auditioning for my first role in community theater. My great latent self had guided me to the theater, and I had always wanted to appear on stage, but I was so nervous during my first audition that I could not even remember the words. I went completely blank.

"This was very difficult because I had practiced for two weeks straight. I knew every word by heart, but when I stepped onto the stage, everything was gone. I felt so embarrassed.

"It was as if my ego and my great latent self were splitting apart and I was nobody—not ego, not great latent self—nobody.

"Somehow I stayed calm. I focused my breathing and reminded myself that I was on the open path. Out of nowhere, it seems, my lines reappeared, and I gave a performance that shocked even me.

"Through staying calm, I invited my great latent self to give that performance. I was thrilled to have landed my first role in community theater."

· · ·

Stella's experience reveals the power of meeting challenges with calm. Her story is a wonderful illustration of how being dedicated to the open path can move us powerfully into our lives.

We can use Stella's example as we experience our everyday lives. By meeting every challenge with calm, we can discover consistency in our lives. Stella was searching for a consistency that could only come from her great latent self, a depth that appears when we make room for it.

We make space for our great latent self when we live out of it more often, when we do not allow our ego to be in charge.

One area where our great latent self can be present but where we seldom invite it to operate is in our daily routines: doing laundry and dishes, grocery shopping, cooking, cleaning, and getting ready for work. This is where our great latent self can thrive. By streamlining these activities into organized rituals, we will begin to love routines.

When the great latent self is present in our mundane lives, we increase our capacity to stay on the open path. Through this capacity, we reduce feeling overwhelmed, slow our pace, and more often use our practices to stay connected to our great latent self and the sphere of genius.

Weariness is a sign that ego has
regained control of your life.

Protect Your Drive

It takes drive to stay on the open path and climb the mountain. How much drive do you have? Your answer may surprise you. Your ego may tell you that your drive is limited, that you do not have the energy or motivation for the climb, but your great latent self possesses a drive that is limitless.

Your great latent self could climb the mountain hundreds of times in one lifetime and still be as fresh as a marathoner at the beginning of a race.

Protect your drive. Beware of weariness. Weariness is a sign that ego has regained control of your life. Be aware of boredom, another sign that your ego is suffocating your great latent self.

Beware of the seduction of the term *fine*, through which your ego is keeping you limited. It will tell you that your life is just fine when in reality you haven't even begun to live it fully.

· · ·

"I allowed the seduction of *fine* to limit me for an entire decade after college," Rachel explains. "I thought it was fine to have a meaningless job as long as I was working. I would go out with my friends, but I could not spend much money, or I wouldn't have enough for my rent at the beginning of the next month. Somehow I thought that was fine too.

"If I had given in to the seduction of fine, I would never have the life I have now. I love traveling, being an exciting part of a team, and enjoying social activities."

· · ·

"If I had given in to the seduction of fine," Stella recalls, "I would not have gotten to the theater in the first place or begun acting on stage. I would have been trapped in my old, limited life because it was fine, but what amazes me more than anything is that acting on stage was not my deepest desire. Being a doctor was.

"Somehow I had to act on stage to even consider the possibility of entertaining my deepest desire, that of being a doctor. The seduction of fine would have taken me away from so much beauty in my life. I would never have met my husband. I would not have the life I have now."

· · ·

By protecting our drive and using it fully, we are connecting with our great latent self. We will always have enough energy to do all the things that are important in our lives. We will avoid mountaintop dead ends.

By avoiding the seduction of fine, we will remain on the open path.

Relish Your Vitality

Challenges on the open path often come about when our vitality is low. High vitality is a sign that we are connected to our great latent self and the sphere of genius. Mountaintop prosperity and vitality go hand in hand. Traveling the open path gives us greater vitality.

· · ·

"When I first stepped onto the open path," Audrey says, "I was very weak. I had not been eating right, my sleep was tentative, and I was exhausted. When the open path appeared, I did not have a lot of stamina. I did, however, notice a significant increase in my vitality.

"Even though my physical body was a mess from all the stress and grief, my vitality picked up immediately. My friends commented that a spark came back to my eyes. I felt connected to the power that I now recognize as universal flow. My hope meter's needle was almost instantaneously pushing toward high. That came from vitality, not stamina. It took me months to build stamina, but the vitality I experienced immediately."

. . .

Our vitality can be measured every moment. It is a barometer for how connected we are to our great latent self. When we relish our vitality, challenges on the open path are not insurmountable. We become confident that we can resolve the issues that arise.

> *Let the spirit of your future pull you toward greater prosperity. Be all in.*

Partner with Your Future

The sphere of genius holds a portal to your future, and through your great latent self, you have access to that portal. By partnering with your future—really committing to it—you will be able to look ahead months and years and know where you are going by the resonance you feel today.

The sixth breakthrough on the open path, mountaintop resonance, allows you to tap into the sphere of genius, acquiring sonar as you do. You can use that sonar to ensure that you are in resonant alignment with your future. Mountaintop resonance is not only about now—it is about the life you are creating in the future.

Let the spirit of your future pull you toward greater prosperity. *Be all in.* You must be so committed to your future on the mountaintop that your life is not vague. You are fully committed, and you know exactly what you are fully committed to.

When you partner with your future, you will naturally celebrate both overcoming the challenges on your open path and your mountaintop breakthroughs. You will notice that the bumps on the open path are really opportunities to become stronger and better and more prepared to continue your travels up the mountain.

With your great latent self present to decode messages from your challenges, you will be amazed at how quickly your challenges resolve and how ingenious the resolutions will be.

Chapter Seven

Develop a Triumphant Approach

On the open path, your sense of security comes from three things:

1. Your connection to your great latent self.
2. Through your great latent self, your connection to the sphere of genius.
3. Your commitment to the open path.

When you understand that your security comes from these three things, you will naturally develop a triumphant approach to life. This approach leads you to recognize that your great latent self is a truer definition of who you are, and you will no longer take your ego's fears seriously. Your great latent self has then prevailed over your ego's fears.

Your triumphant approach to life can be streamed. It is a way of engaging life from the viewpoint of a winner. It is about showing up fully and preparing for success without getting locked into a small definition of what that means. A triumphant approach is about giving yourself credit for putting one foot in front of the other in climbing the mountain, knowing there may be wins and losses along the way. The real win is that you remain on the open path.

A triumphant approach allows you to avoid the high costs associated with succumbing to the fears of the ego. These costs can be measured in lost time, lost opportunities, loss of money, loss of creativity, and illness. The costs are real and will set us back in all these areas. A triumphant approach allows you to avoid the costs of succumbing to the fears of the ego even when the open path gets bumpy.

Recall Past Triumphs

"That day when my mind went blank auditioning for my part in the play," recalls Stella, "was very painful until my great latent self came forward. I had to manage the tension of that blank space when my ego pulled away and my great latent self was nowhere in sight.

"I had to stay in that moment of blankness for what seemed like an eternity, but then a memory came to me. I recalled being in acting class in junior high, and even though I did not have a major role, I remembered how fun it was. The thought just came to me.

"I was one of the monkeys in the *Wizard of Oz*. That was a past triumph. I felt so proud during those performances. It was that memory that brought my great latent self back to the stage. I saved the audition by recalling my junior high triumph. I was calling my great latent self back to my life."

. . .

Mountaintop prosperity is born out of triumphs. Whether the triumph is based on prevailing, succeeding, and winning; merely living with our great latent self fully present; or convincing ourselves that we deserve mountaintop prosperity in the first place, we climb the open path one triumph at a time.

When we recall past triumphs, we do exactly what Stella described: we call our great latent self back. Our experience of victory is a way of inviting our great latent self to be fully present.

Mountaintop prosperity is born out of triumphs.

One way to increase your triumphant approach is to keep a triumph diary. Bring a memory of the experience of winning and being triumphant into the present so that you can recall how it feels. Use your recollections to encourage your great latent self to be more fully present on a daily basis. List your triumphs, your successes, your victories, your wins. Recall them, each one in vivid detail. These memories will help you stay on the open path.

Get and Stay Unstuck

We get stuck when we venture off the open path. Once we have fallen away from the open path, ego will use resistance to keep us from reconnecting with our great latent self. We have reached a dead end, and it is our resistance that keeps us stuck.

Ego is the maker of all resistance. Its apathy and paralysis can be incredibly powerful, so much so that it can keep us stuck for an entire lifetime.

What are some things that you tell yourself that keep you stuck? A common misconception relates to visibility on the open path. As our life becomes more ours and we allow our great latent self to lead the way, we naturally become more visible to others. Ego will confuse visibility with vulnerability and try to keep us from being all in.

When you fear visibility because you confuse it with vulnerability, you will not allow yourself to stand out as a distinct individual, and your great latent self will not be fully present. You will fear being vulnerable to attack, but it need not be so.

The visibility of your great latent self is actually quite protective. Being tapped into the sphere of genius will help you know when to showcase your mountaintop drive and prosperity and when to remain present and visible but not overtly influential.

When you are stuck in resistance for any reason, your past is limiting you. Your personal story is a detriment to your progress in life. It is important to transform your personal story by finding the now. In other words, what is the truth right now?

> *It is important to transform your personal story*
> *by finding the now.*

Being stuck may take on different forms. You may decide that it is no longer important to reach the mountaintop, and you may even think that your great latent self is speaking, but in reality ego is telling you that your life is not important.

You may decide that it is too hard, that you want to forget about your big ideas, that you do not have the time or money or stamina to go after what you really want. All of this is resistance. The truth is that life will go on. Whether you are traveling the open path or checked out as if it doesn't matter, the same amount of time will have passed.

In one scenario, you might find yourself stuck on a dead end indefinitely. In another scenario, you might have followed the open path, learned many great lessons, and had many mountaintop breakthroughs. You might be enjoying the discoveries of who you really are and what you are really made of.

Regardless of how difficult it becomes, staying on the open path will give you more to show for your life than resisting and staying stuck on a dead end.

The quickest way to get and stay unstuck is to move into meaningful action, action prompted by your great latent self and guided by the sphere of genius. Action may involve picking up the phone to make one phone call, or it may lead you to take a class or invest in a business.

Take action that keeps you on the open path, resonating with the sphere of genius and moving toward mountaintop identification. There you will once again understand that the sphere of genius is within you, and it will always guide you to release your resistance.

Develop a habit of saying yes. While ego's favorite word is *no*, the great latent self's favorite word is yes! Look for opportunities to say yes, and say yes more often. Each yes is another step on the open path. Say yes to greater potential, greater possibility. Say yes to greater opportunities. Say yes to greater connections. Say yes to life.

Cultivate Your Strengths

Your strengths connect you to the open mountaintop path: the strength in your drive, your strength of will, the strength of your yes, the strength of your great latent self. It takes strength to be on the open path, and your personal strengths must be cultivated.

While athletes may dream of a medal, their only chance of getting one is through developing their strengths.

Developing our strength is not about wishing and hoping. It is about the actual, real development of our being.

. . .

"I did not realize how weak I was," Audrey says. "I thought I was a strong person for having made it through a difficult life and surviving so much heartbreak, but that did not prepare me for the open path.

"It was my ego that survived difficulties and heartbreak, while my great latent self had been waiting patiently for me to connect. Had I known about the open path sooner, my great latent self may have saved me from tremendous heartbreak.

"Once I got onto the open path and stepped farther and farther away from being too selfless, I discovered how weak I really was. But I knew I had to become strong for the open path.

"I needed to become strong in my speech to set boundaries, to say no. I needed to be strong in my concept of myself and remember that I was my great latent self.

"I needed to be strong in my physical body, because I was so depleted by giving myself away.

"I needed to strengthen my mind, because my mind had become as small as my world. Painfully small.

"Today I am strong. I read the news, and it no longer devastates me. I think more about ways I can help instead of allowing it to make me feel helpless.

"I exercise several times a week, and I am amazed at the strength in my body.

"I can say no today, and I do not even need to have a good reason. I can say no just because I do not feel like saying yes. My no is not about being too selfish. I know all of the ways I say yes and all of the ways I help. My no is my great latent self guiding me.

"It is funny how being stronger in my ability to say no has also made my yes so much stronger. The strength of my great latent self has shown up on every level of my life."

. . .

Developing our strength is not about wishing and hoping. It is about the actual, real development of our being.

What strengths do you need to develop for the open path? Like Audrey, many people on the open path need to cultivate the strength of their mind, body, spirit, and even their presence. The strength of their commitment and resolve must also be developed.

What strengths do you already have? Our great latent self is strong. As we make more room for it in our lives, we will become stronger too. We will naturally gravitate toward activities and experiences that build our strength.

Commit to the Open Path

"When I applied for medical school," Stella recalls, "it was the biggest commitment I had ever made. Perhaps I committed so strongly because it was such a stretch for me to believe it was actually possible to become a doctor, and I was not sure I would be successful.

"I took the commitment to my marriage just as seriously, but it did not scare me the same way that applying for medical school did. For me, my marriage was about security. It wasn't hard to commit to the security I found with my husband. I felt supported on the open path with him, but medical school was different.

"Before I started, staying on the open path in medical school seemed like an impossibility. How could I possibly make room for my great latent self when I would be so busy with my studies? How could I resonate with the sphere of genius when my mind would be full of academic exercises and studying for tests?

"I had a notion that academics, having originated from humans and often presented by professors with big egos, would block the sphere of genius, but I stayed dedicated to the open path as I applied for medical school. I was amazed at how often I resonated with the sphere of genius through my studies and experiences.

"I even became a favorite with my professors because I seemed to know what they were trying to get across. It seemed that they were also connected to the sphere of genius. If I had not been on the open path, I would never have recognized that.

"My mountaintop message changed in medical school. It became a message about commitment and how important it is to commit to the open path. The open path will appear in every situation if we let it. It will appear where we least expect it. When we are committed to the open path, mountaintop prosperity is always within reach in one form or another."

Aspire to Excellence

A triumphant approach means striving to surpass ordinary standards. When we strive for excellence, we are allowing our great
latent self to be more present in our life and show us what we
are really capable of.

When we strive for excellence, we are on the open path. It
is not about perfection or pressure. It is about reaching for our
great latent self and giving it a voice in our lives.

. . .

"For me, striving for excellence was about caring for my
mother in a different way. Before I discovered the open path, I
carried a lot of resentment," Audrey says. "As a caregiver, your
job is never done. Fixing meals and doing laundry made me
feel so small.

"I had always felt responsible for my mother. The older she
got, the more I was reminded of my own life wasting away. It
was a terrible situation because, of course, she could not really
be happy while I carried so much resentment. Even though I
never said a word about it, I'm sure she felt it. She knew I was
giving her my life.

> *A triumphant approach means striving*
> *to surpass ordinary standards.*

"When I committed to the open path, everything changed.
My resentment vanished. I felt lucky to have the opportunity
to care for my mother, whom I loved so much. I began using a
standard of excellence and watched how it completely changed
the tone in my household.

"With my great latent self present, I realized how much power
I had to lift everyone's spirits. I just needed to make sure I was
not wasting my life in the process.

"I had let go of a job that was draining when I found the

open path years before. For years I took care of my mother full time before beginning to work for a nonprofit that helps less-than-privileged kids do better in school. I was with them until recently, and it was great and fulfilling work for me. When I started my own nonprofit and began receiving grants for after school teen empowerment programs, my life went to a completely new level.

"Money was never the most important thing to me, but I was able to make enough money to bring in some support at home so that I could focus on helping more kids become empowered and find the open path. Helping children in this way, especially teens, is completely exhilarating. It all started because I chose to aspire to excellence, and now I teach others to do the same."

Believe in Your Great Latent Self

Your great latent self carries potential for mountaintop prosperity. Whether you have made contact with your great latent self at this point is not important. Holding the intention to connect with your great latent self will naturally take you there.

Look for your great latent self to show up in your life by recalling past triumphs, noticing when you emerge above the fog, developing a triumphant approach, and partnering with your future. These are all ways to cultivate your great latent self. The more you cultivate your presence in this way, the more your life will continue to unfold, and the open path will be revealed.

While reaching the mountaintop may come and go in your life, your great latent self is real and constant. The sphere of genius is within you, even if you don't hold onto this truth every minute of every day. Understand that your great latent self is unfolding and will always lead you back to the mountaintop.

Regardless of where you are on the open path, you will never reach the end of discovering your great latent self. There are always new surprises that reveal your great latent self and who you really are. Your great latent self operates in the sphere of genius, and the sphere of genius created the entire universe.

Remember that your great latent self streams universal intelligence, and by listening to this higher intelligence, your life will forever change. Your great latent self is and has always been inside you. It is your biggest fan.

Chapter Eight

Stoke the Fire in Your Belly

You can keep the memory of the open path alive when you stoke the fire in your belly. Recall times of great passion on the open path, and use your memory to keep that passion alive.

Along with your triumph diary, begin a passion diary. Passion taps into your personal energy in a timeless way. By recalling a past passion, you have access to that personal energy right now.

. . .

Rachel recalls how she fell in love with life, and she is still in love with life today. She has kept her passion alive for many years on the open path by recalling over and over again the way falling in love with life allowed her great latent self to be present.

. . .

For Stella, it was performing at the theater. "I have never felt so alive," Stella says. "I will never forget the moment when we stood in a line holding hands and bowing after that first production. The audience was clapping, and I did not think I could smile any bigger.

"It is true that I was holding my husband's hand. He had also performed in the production, but this was before our first date. I did think he was cute and funny, but I never imagined that we would end up married. With the passion I felt, my great latent self must have known I would marry him. It is the only thing that explains the enormous passion I experienced that night. I think of it often because it keeps the fire in my belly stoked."

. . .

Just one memory can lead us back to the open path to the mountaintop. Having these memories close by is a way to keep ourselves pointed in the right direction and away from dead ends.

Come up with a collection of mountaintop memories and then create a mountaintop-memory recall practice. Meditate on the memories and experience them fully: the passion, the awe, the wonder, the power. Resonate with these memories as a way to move into harmony with them on the open path.

Add memories to your mountaintop memory collection regularly.

Embrace Your Mountaintop Desires

What are your mountaintop desires? Now is a good time to think about them in detail. What do you want on the mountaintop? What is important to your life? Be creative with your answer. See it in vivid color.

Keep a journal and scrapbook for your mountaintop desires. Cut out pictures from magazines that represent those desires. Keep your collections handy. Revisit them often, and you'll be amazed at how quickly they manifest in your life.

Mountaintop prosperity is about plenty. If your personal story tells you that desire is a bad thing, your great latent self will remind you that it is not. Mountaintop desires are not shallow.

They do not come from the ego but from the great latent self. For that reason, they will benefit all.

Your deepest desires form your map on the open path. It is your desire that pulls you into your future at the top of the mountain. Your desire is motivating you for the climb each day.

When your desires come from your great latent self, they are deep desires. They have power and potency and meaning. Once you arrive on the mountaintop with greater resources and greater personal energy, you will realize that your desire is good and should be embraced.

What is important to your life?

A child who desires a lollipop is not looked upon as bad even though the lollipop offers no nutritional value. The sweetness of the lollipop is a reward. We also need to be rewarded for staying on the open path. Even if the reward has little substance, the act of rewarding ourselves is nourishment alone.

As long as you stay on the open path, you needn't worry about your desires taking you to a dead end. They will balance on their own. At times you will desire sweet but superficial experiences; at other times, you will want a full, nutritious meal.

Allow your desires to become your map on the open path. They are a reflection of you, and embracing them will prepare you to embrace the joys and pleasures ahead.

See Yourself on the Mountaintop

Envision yourself on the mountaintop. Make it real. What will the mountaintop look like for you? Does it include a beautiful home, a nice car, money, friends, community, travel, quality time with loved ones, engaging work, fulfilling hobbies, or making a difference in the world?

Envision yourself there and notice how you feel. Choose the existence that feels positive.

Stella got through medical school by seeing herself on her mountaintop with the life she has now. She had to choose it over and over again when encountering bumps on the path and through a dead end or two. She chose it repeatedly no matter what happened along the way.

Make seeing yourself on the mountaintop a habit, a consciously created habit. Make seeing yourself on the mountaintop your *first* conscious habit.

Victory—standing on the mountaintop with your hands in the air—is a powerful and valuable emotion. Like triumph, victory is a favorite emotion of our great latent self. At a deep level, we are naturally victorious. The personal energy we access through victory can be put to use in our daily lives.

Use the energy of victory to keep your daily life flowing on the open path until your great latent self has grown powerful enough to claim victory as a natural state of being.

Direct Your Mountaintop Passion

Mountaintop passion is real and immense, and it must be directed responsibly. When we stoke the fire in our belly, our mountaintop passion will build, sometimes to a boiling point.

Our mountaintop passion must be directed toward our goals. The great latent self will be filled with passion, but we must make that passion translate into real accomplishment. For this, we must get the ego to cooperate.

As you remember, the ego was formed when we were young, mainly due to fear of our environment. Until we discover the open path, our ego keeps our great latent self dormant. On the open path, however, our great latent self gains momentum and our desires build.

This is a good sign, but our passion must transform our ego, because even though we are no longer living from it, the ego is still our gate to the outer world. We need to move through that gate in order to create mountaintop prosperity.

At first, the ego will try to steal our passion and suffocate our great latent self, because that is all it knows how to do. As we act on our intention to turn the ego around to face the world rather than letting it close in on us, we begin to reshape the ego as a supporter rather than a suppressor of our dreams.

Ego as a supporter will help us manage our passion and direct it into the world in a successful way. When our mountaintop passion is directed, our great latent self will find a friend in the ego—an assistant, a great supporter. We will find ways to make room for more mountaintop passion in our daily lives. Once that happens, the ego can no longer rule us through fear.

Celebrate Mountaintop Success

Mountaintop success can be large or small. It can be as simple as taking the time to meditate in the morning or as significant as buying a new house. Each mountaintop success, regardless of how large or small it is, must be celebrated.

This does not necessarily mean that we need to go out and celebrate with others. Often our mountaintop successes can be celebrated internally. The important thing is to witness another success.

When we celebrate our mountaintop successes, our great latent self becomes more present in our lives. The more we take notice of our great latent self, the more our great latent self shows up. Each success encourages our great latent self to show up more and more often in our lives.

Each mountaintop success, regardless of how large or small it is, must be celebrated.

Celebrating with others, however, is as powerful as celebrating internally. When we celebrate with others, the community experience amplifies the recognition of our great latent self, bringing more energy to the open path.

A celebratory attitude can be carried into daily life. We can celebrate the sunrise, the rain, grass growing, or birds chirping. On the open path, celebration is natural.

A celebratory attitude attracts greater prosperity. It keeps our great latent self present, connects us to the sphere of genius, and opens the hope portal to our future.

Celebration is a beneficial practice to adopt for mountaintop prosperity. Each day we can choose to celebrate not only our own successes but the successes of others, along with the unlimited successes in the natural world.

Clarify Your Mountaintop Goals

Invite your great latent self to participate fully in your daily life and stream your future. You have seen yourself on the mountaintop, embraced your mountaintop desires, learned how to direct your mountaintop passion, and celebrated your mountaintop successes. It is now time to clarify your mountaintop goals.

Begin to develop a timeline to take you into your future. Take your vision from the mountaintop and ask yourself what it will take to get there. What will you need to do along the way to make it a reality? Do not let your ego suffocate your great latent self. Let your great latent self have the floor.

Your great latent self, remember, is connected to the sphere of genius. It is the sphere of genius that keeps the entire universe in motion and our ecosphere perfectly balanced. It can certainly guide you to your mountaintop.

Developing your timeline will help you create a map of your desires and turn it into a plan for success. Of course your map of desires will change as you step forward on the open path, but by bringing clarity to your desires and mountaintop goals, you will begin to locate where you currently are in your life and in which direction you need to move.

By creating your map of desires, the kind of life you want, who you may be connected to, what your network may look like, who your friends may be, how your life may evolve, and how you may use your prosperity to make your life better will be revealed to you.

Together, your map of desires and your timeline lead to the steps for creating mountaintop prosperity, which will become more and more apparent. Your great latent self is connected to the sphere of genius and will nudge you in the right direction. You will then be carrying the mountaintop flame into your life.

If you get to the top of the mountain and become careless or lazy or think that the path does not continue to unfold forever, you can easily lose your mountaintop prosperity.

Keep Your Mountaintop Spark Alive

Reaching the top of the mountain will seem familiar to you. While the journey is real, the challenges difficult, and the effort demanding, reaching the mountaintop may be a surprisingly simple experience.

Even though staying on the open path is one of the most difficult things you will ever do, manifesting mountaintop prosperity will seem natural. You will find yourself driving that new car, working in that new position, owning that new business, taking those exciting vacations, or putting your feet on sandy beaches. It all becomes effortless once you have cracked the code and followed the open path all the way to the mountaintop.

Your challenge now is to keep the mountaintop spark alive.

You must keep your life in order to keep the spark alive. If you get to the top of the mountain and become careless or lazy or think that the path does not continue to unfold forever, you can easily lose your mountaintop prosperity.

How will you keep your spark alive when you reach the mountaintop? Knowing that your great latent self must always take the lead over your ego is an important part of the answer to this question.

You can also keep your spark alive by developing a mountain-top spark meter. Check in with yourself on a daily basis and ask, "How is my mountaintop spark? How creative am I feeling? Is my success interfering with my drive?"

Hold the intention of keeping your mountaintop spark alive. Build your capacity to keep it alive. Use your triumphant approach to keep it alive. Do whatever you need to do to keep your spark glowing.

Another idea for keeping your mountaintop spark alive is to create a mountaintop success team, a team of your personal supporters with whom you can discuss your mountaintop goals and who can suggest new ways to keep the spark alive.

Your success team will most likely encourage you to look for your next mountaintop challenge, because mountaintop pros-perity is a self-fulfilling prophecy. It needs to keep expanding.

PART III

Living Mountaintop Prosperity

Chapter Nine

Surrender to the Highest Good

The open path requires that we engage in life in a new way. We need to focus completely on the steps ahead and also surrender to the highest good ... at the same time. The open path teaches us this new way of being.

Surrender Through Curiosity

We surrender to the highest good when we surrender to our curiosity. We no longer need to have all the answers. We can allow our curiosity to keep us engaged and not desperately attached to anything. The truth is that life changes each day, and desperate attachment is a child of the ego. Curiosity, on the other hand, is a child of the great latent self.

Through mountaintop sonar, we will *feel* the highest good. We will sense which actions, decisions, and even thoughts are the highest actions, decisions, and thoughts.

Our curiosity will take us beyond what we already know into new questions, into thinking outside the box and playing with new ways of thinking about life.

Through curiosity we will reach new heights by discovering places in our minds and hearts that we ever knew before.

Our Amphibious Nature

By surrendering to the highest good, we discover our amphibious nature. We learn that at times it's important to walk the shore in life, steadily putting one foot in front of the other. At other times on the open path, we need to jump into the stream and let it carry us. We must learn to surrender to the current.

Our amphibious nature allows us to be both steadfast in our approach and fluid when flexibility is needed. By the time we have experienced the third breakthrough, mountaintop inspiration, our amphibious nature has begun to develop. Our inspiration creates a fluidity in us that allows us to make great strides in very little time and with very little effort.

We continue to discover and trust our amphibious nature by the fourth breakthrough, mountaintop recognition. We learn that the open path is taking us to the highest good—to the mountaintop.

The seventh breakthrough, mountaintop streaming, is all about using our amphibious nature. We tap into the stream of universal flow. We float on the currents of universal intelligence, discovering more about life every moment.

We discover through our amphibious nature that we can step out of the current and onto the earth, bringing universal intelligence into our daily lives: our work, our meetings, our creative pursuits, our business ventures, our relationships. Our amphibious nature allows us to live in a way we never thought possible.

Mountaintop prosperity is a byproduct of a mountaintop life. It is an expression of the life we are living within.

Trust is Our Birthright

Trust is more than a concept; it is a crucial component of our great latent self. In other words, it is already woven into who we are and who we are becoming. Our great latent self knows trust. The ego does not.

Ego does not trust life, and it does not trust us, so it keeps us very small. The ego does not want us to know that trust is our birthright, that it is already woven into our cells at a very deep level, a level inhabited by our great latent self. Infants trust that they will be cared for; they must trust for survival.

Trust is more than a concept; it is a crucial
component of our great latent self.

Trust is like a golden thread of purity, and it carries the spark of life. When our great latent self is present, our cells are dancing with trust in ourselves, in the universe, and in all of life. Trust shapes how our cells process the information that influences our behavior.

On the open path, it is trust that calms our fight-or-flight responses. If the path gets bumpy, trust allows us to stay on the path even though we cannot see beyond the bend. It was trust that allowed Audrey to listen to the calm that came over her while she was wailing in grief.

Trust allows us to surrender to the highest good. When we utter the words, "I do not trust," we cut ourselves off from the purest part of ourselves and from our great latent self and the sphere of genius.

Trust allows us to surrender to the highest good.

If you have difficulty trusting in life, understand that the open path will naturally take you to greater trust.

The Magic of Momentum
When we understand that surrendering to the highest good means being fluid, we begin to live life with a greater sense of momentum. We intuitively understand that we must protect this momentum at all costs.

We understand that this protection is not about building fortresses. It is about the tenacious pursuit of the mountaintop. It is about the uncompromising belief in our ability to travel all the way to the top through natural momentum on the open path.

Momentum on the open path is a sign that our great latent self is tapped into the sphere of genius and supporting our every step. Our vision and partnership with our future pulls us toward it. Every cell in our body awakens to opportunities we are allowing ourselves to explore.

> *When our great latent self is present,*
> *it animates our being.*

Ego no longer dominates. We have adopted a triumphant approach to life, and we are experiencing the deep security that can only come from the sphere of genius and the open path.

Stay on the Creative Wave

Our next task is to stay on the creative wave. The open path is a creative path, a path where our great latent self is free to create. Staying on the creative wave allows us to build mountaintop prosperity quickly. On the creative wave, we can have more—more money, more friendship, more engagement with life, more fun, more meaning, more of whatever we choose.

The Glow of Surrender

When we surrender to the highest good, we take on a glow because we have allowed our great latent self to be present in our lives. When our great latent self is present, it animates our being. The sphere of genius shines through us. We take on a childlike vitality regardless of our age.

The glow of surrender is not about letting go of anything. It is not about giving up anything. It is about claiming everything.

As counterintuitive as it may seem, we must surrender our

way up the mountain on the open path. We must allow universal flow to carry us.

Watch Your Life Unfold

When we surrender to the highest good and allow universal flow to carry us, we see our life unfold in ways we never thought possible. The people we meet, the places we go, and the experiences we have all seem incredible to us.

As we surrender to our highest good, our great latent self is given permission to inhabit our life, and ego cannot stop us. As we watch our lives unfold, all of what is good and pure and true about us has an opportunity to live. In that joy, we find meaning and fulfillment we never thought possible.

Chapter Ten

Cultivate Your Courage to Love

An intense love of life awaits our arrival on the mountain-top. Our great latent self is finally free to speak in its native tongue, a universal love language. The sphere of genius is a loyal inner guide, and we realize that on the mountaintop our only task is to be fully present. It is time to explore what love really is and how to use it in the world of ordinary affairs.

Mountaintop love—like the mysterious world it comes from—has many dimensions. It's other-worldly nature opens us to universal flow so powerfully that not only do we want to take the best life has to offer, but we want to *give* our best and contribute to a healthy world.

Mountaintop Prosperity is Love

Mountaintop prosperity is love in all its varied forms. It compels us to bring our great latent self out of dormancy to lean into life, swim the oceans, dive off cliffs, study and develop ourselves, and look for solutions to our personal and planetary problems.

. . .

"Mountaintop prosperity brought me so much more than I could have ever imagined," Stella explains. "I thought it would just bring me people who understood me so that I would have friends to talk to. I wasn't even expecting a great career and marriage.

"I did not even think to want more than that, but approaching the top of the mountain and realizing in a visceral way that the sphere of genius is within me opened my heart to so much love that my career took on an amazing new dimension.

Mountaintop prosperity is a byproduct of a mountaintop life. It is an expression of the life we are living within.

"I am not just helping my patients because I can. I am helping them because I love them. My love extends to everything. I have discovered mountaintop love."

Mountaintop Love is a Glue
"When I decided to work at the nonprofit, I was afraid my family would fall apart," Audrey says. "I had done everything for so long that I didn't think my kids could get along without me always there. I did bring help in for my mother, but what amazed me more than anything was the love that showed up as I resonated and streamed and appreciated glimpses of the mountaintop. My being on the open path actually brought my family closer together in love."

. . .

Becoming more aware of the real power of love is common as we approach the mountaintop. We watch as the momentum of life begins to orbit around our great latent self. This is not an egoic statement. The ego has surrendered; it has collapsed. This positive orbit is a natural phenomenon related to the collapse of the ego. And it is not just one orbit. There are orbits among orbits. Whenever the great latent self is free from the ego, an orbit of love is created. Our lives naturally move into order.

Mountaintop Love is a Motivator

Rachel used the motivational power of mountaintop love when her open path became bumpy. As she explains, it took over a year for her to find the right job, and she would never have been able to remain fresh and eager for every interview if mountaintop love hadn't been streaming through the open path.

Rachel's openness to mountaintop love allowed her to stay tapped into the sphere of genius. She took it seriously, and it changed her life. The motivating force of mountaintop love kept Rachel going until she secured her new position. It freed her from being trapped.

• • •

Stella also experienced mountaintop love as a motivator in her life. "I think I had always known the love at the top of the mountain," Stella says, "but I didn't use it for motivation until I got a glimpse of the open path. I was so afraid that I would be lonely, that even though I knew there was love at the top, I did not know if that love would be personal or if I would be alone in my own world with a sense of love for life.

"When I let mountaintop love motivate me to step onto the open path, I immediately felt less lonely. I realized to my surprise that my loneliness was much greater before I had stepped onto the open path even though I had people and family around me. Because they did not understand me, my loneliness was nearly unbearable. I realized that the open path is all about letting love into our lives."

Aspiration is Mountaintop Self-Love

The ego says it is useless for us to aspire in life. It cripples aspiration with its critical voice, which promotes the notion that aspiration and over-ambition are the same thing. The ego warns us that aspiration will lead to selfishness and greed.

This is another lie that the ego believes and uses to keep us small and protected from the big, dangerous world of ego's domain. The truth is that aspiration is mountaintop self-love, a type of love that honors life itself.

When we aspire to excellence—to bring our great latent self out of dormancy and develop ourselves—we discover the power of mountaintop self-love.

. . .

The truth is that aspiration is mountaintop self-love, a type of love that honors life itself.

"One day I realized staying in that small job year after year as a customer service rep, where all I did was speak on the phone all day, was really causing self-harm," Rachel says. "I got a glimpse of what self-love is all about. It was about going after the life I really wanted. This discovery on the open path is when everything changed. I realized that when we aspire to be great, we are experiencing self-love."

"It is not just a thought," she explains. "It is deeper than a thought. It is a truth. Aspiration really is mountaintop self-love."

Rachel went on to talk about her desire for more money on the open path:

"Money is important to me, and when I allowed that to be true and aspired not only to develop myself in terms of my knowledge and skill but to develop my ability to earn more money, it opened a gate for me. I suddenly saw my desire as self-love.

"I realized that for so many years I felt like a racehorse pushed behind the starting gate. I was holding myself back. When I stepped onto the open path, my aspirations were freed. I could run on the open path forever. Life could be a thrilling adventure." When I stepped onto the open path, my aspirations were freed. I could run on the open path forever. Life could be a thrilling adventure.

. . .

When we move beyond feeling guilty for wanting more or feeling afraid that we will become greedy or selfish, our aspirations are freed. We've finally given our great latent self room to run free.

Recover Pure Mountaintop Love

When we get a glimpse that the mountaintop is all about love, we may recall all the times in our life that we loved fully. Even if these times were tarnished by trauma, our pure love played an important part in the people we have become today.

Love that survives trauma is pure. And pure love accumulates over a lifetime. The ego will try to make us forget about the times we loved openly and freely. To the ego, the risk is too great and the pain too real if our love doesn't last a lifetime. Ego wants to protect us from loss.

Our great latent self doesn't need protection. It is tapped into the sphere of genius and knows at a very deep level that loss is part of the human experience. We are made to survive loss. We are not made to live without love. Our task on the mountaintop is to recover our ability to love and to recover it fully.

Recall the times when you felt pure love in your life. Perhaps this was with a grandmother or an elder in your community or your parents or family. Look for all of the times in your life when you felt it fully, even if for just a moment.

String those moments together and create a design of pure mountaintop love. Every moment you can think of in your life that was pure was when your great latent self was present to experience love fully. Remember those moments. Hold them sacred.

When you hold this design sacred, you are telling the universe you understand. You are free from the ego's hold and are able to explore—really explore—the power of mountaintop love.

Keep a mountaintop love journal. Add experiences of pure love to it regularly. Keep developing your design of pure mountaintop love forever.

Turn Grudges into Mountaintop Gratitude

Stella talks about grudges. "I was so surprised to discover that I was holding grudges. I did not even know I had them," she says. "I knew I was unfulfilled with my friends and family and never felt understood, but I did not realize how much anger I had toward them until I stepped onto the open path and started creating my own life.

"I noticed that even though I was happier than ever, I was also more intolerant than ever. The open path led me to understand that I had many grudges toward those who could not relate to me.

"It took me a long time, but little by little I was able to turn my grudges into mountaintop gratitude. I became grateful that they didn't understand me because if they had, I wouldn't have been motivated to discover my own life. I wouldn't have been motivated to join the theater and become a doctor. I wouldn't have met my husband.

"When I was able to see that, I let go of my grudges. I was filled with mountaintop gratitude."

· · ·

Audrey says, "I don't think it will surprise you to hear that I was filled with grudges. I knew I was, even at the time. I even held grudges toward my husbands before they had their affairs. I was a very resentful person.

"It took me a long time to let go of my grudges. It took understanding that the space where I was holding a grudge was keeping my great latent self from being fully present. I began to understand how important it was to let go of my grudges and move into gratitude.

"I cannot say that I am grateful that my husbands had affairs and that my marriages failed, but I am grateful to have been pushed so low in life that my great latent self and the sphere of genius stepped in to guide me. I would never have found my own way. I would always have been selfless and resentful."

. . .

The ego is known for holding onto grudges forever.
It does so in the name of self-protection, but the
sad fact is that our grudges make us weak.
They drain us on every level.

"For me," Rachel says, "my grudges transformed quickly to mountaintop gratitude. I do not really hold grudges. I never have. In fact, I had to look for my grudges.

"Nobody made me stay in an unfulfilling job. In fact, my parents always wanted more for me. They did not understand why, after spending so much on college, I would start working in such a low-paying job. Maybe the grudge that I had to let go of was a grudge against myself for accepting so little in my life.

"Either way, the grudge is gone, and my mountaintop gratitude is so big because, as you know, I love my life."

. . .

Most people have grudges they need to release. The ego is known for holding onto grudges forever. It does so in the name of self-protection, but the sad fact is that our grudges make us weak. They drain us on every level.

To create a life of true mountaintop prosperity, we must seek to release grudges in favor of mountaintop gratitude.

Are you currently holding onto grudges in your life? If so, work on releasing them by understanding more fully how the situation you are resentful about actually helped you discover or live on the open path.

Mountaintop Love and Prosperity

When we glimpse that mountaintop love is the power animating the sphere of genius and the entire universe, we understand that mountaintop prosperity is simply a manifestation of identifying with that love. When we know this in our cells, we allow it to animate our life.

The ups and downs on the open path teach us how to manifest mountaintop prosperity through love. We learn not to block it, not to turn away from it, and not to think it is for everyone but us. Opening to love in our lives and manifesting mountaintop prosperity requires that we remember our great latent self, that we bring it out of dormancy to receive the best that life has to offer.

Chapter Eleven

Embrace the World

When you arrive on the mountaintop, you may wonder why it took so long. Your great latent self will validate the fact that manifesting prosperity, while it seems to be the most difficult thing to do in life, is actually not difficult at all. The open path pulls us toward the mountaintop. Manifesting mountaintop prosperity requires that you put one foot in front of the other, and it takes a commitment to the open path.

The real challenge is understanding that we are all in it together and that we each have a role in helping the world get to a better place.

This does not mean we should become selfless. Instead, we should understand that the open path, which leads to mountaintop love, connects all of our great latent selves together. In this mountaintop togetherness are the answers to the world's problems that we will never find alone.

When we accept this truth, we will not be surprised to discover that once we reach the mountaintop, our view opens to new mountains that are higher and more powerful than the one we just climbed. We found mountaintop prosperity for ourselves, but our task is not over.

Discovering a new message about the world on this new mountain is our new task.

Why Your Charisma Matters

Embracing this truth at the top of the mountain feels, in some ways, like we are starting over again. Perhaps we are, but this time we are not starting from the ego. We are starting from our great latent self.

We know we can create through the open path the lives we desire—the fun, the connections, the money, the celebratory approach to life—but the bigger problems of the world have not escaped us.

As counterintuitive as it may seem, it is in the continued opening to that glow of surrender, where the sphere of genius shines through our great latent self, that we will get close to and solve the bigger problems.

Our charisma matters immensely. It's not the charisma of ego but the charisma of the glow of surrender. Through this glow, we can stream with others in magnitudes of personal energy what we cannot stream alone.

Mountaintop streaming in community is our next task, a great new mountain with a great new peak. Discovering a new message about the world on this new mountain is our new task.

Mountaintop Collaboration

When we stream in community, we are exploring that new mountain. We are preparing for a journey we have rarely if ever considered. The eight breakthroughs are before us again. This time, rather than personal breakthroughs, they are community breakthroughs. We must approach them together, all the while knowing we are discovering what it means as we take each step.

When we come together to find the open path in community, we will discover the exponential power of a thousand generations. The power of thousands of beings carrying the power of thousands of generations in thousands of towns will join in discovering how to journey together. Together, we will discover the edge of mountaintop love and understand what our great latent selves can do together that we could never accomplish alone.

Conclusion

Audrey, Stella, and Rachel responded to the question: "Do you live with mountaintop prosperity every day?"

"At this point" Audrey says, "I live with mountaintop prosperity most days but not every day. Once in a while, ego gets a hold of me again and makes me feel small, like I have no right to think big or hope big. But most days I live with mountaintop prosperity. My life is full. I have financial resources and love in my life. The way I think about it, my barometer is now about how much of the time I am exploring that second mountain, the open path to solving even bigger challenges."

. . .

Stella says, "I am aware of my mountaintop prosperity every day. Sometimes when I am tired, I am not as grateful for my busy and full life, but most of the time, my gratitude is overflowing."

. . .

Rachel says, "I do not even think of being on the open path and experiencing mountaintop prosperity every day. It is so much a part of my life that I do not even question it. I just live it. It is so exciting. As you know, I love my life."

PART IV

Support for Your Climb

Chapter Twelve

Mountaintop Prosperity Workbook

The following pages offer quotes from previous chapters along with thought provoking questions. By completing the writing exercises you will discover how to avoid dead ends, stay on the open path and climb to your mountaintop.

Rather than answering the questions in page order, skip around in this section. Skim through the quotes at the top of each page on a regular basis and find one that awakens your great latent self. Give your great latent self a voice and express your deepest truth. Write as much as you'd like and then return at a later date to write more answering the same question. If you'd like, add a date and time to your answers.

By giving careful thought to your answers you will create for yourself a valuable mountaintop map to refer to for years to come.

PART I UNDERSTANDING MOUNTAINTOP PROSPERITY	
KEY POINTS **CHAPTER ONE** **Consider Your Goals**	How Will Your Personal Story Change? How Will Your Views Change? How Will Your Actions Change? Your Greatest Hopes Your Greatest Fears Your Mountaintop Message Imagine Your Life Improving

She couldn't let herself believe that she could be,
in her words, "one of the amazing people in life who
got to be on the open path."

- PAGE 15 -

Do you relate to Stella's story? Is it difficult for you to believe you can be on the open path? How can you strengthen your belief that you can be on the open path?

_____

_____

_____

_____

_____

_____

_____

_____

_____

_____

_____

_____

_____

_____

_____

_____

_____

_____

"I knew at a very deep level everything was going to be okay. I did not know how. I just knew that I did not need to fight so hard, that a path had opened and I would find my way."

- PAGE 16 -

Do you relate to Audrey's story? Describe an experience of knowing at a deep level that everything was going to be okay.

_____

_____

_____

_____

_____

_____

_____

_____

_____

_____

_____

_____

_____

_____

_____

_____

_____

While the path is always there, it can be
truly experienced only when we have a
sincere willingness to follow it

- PAGE 16 -

Describe your sincere willingness to follow the open path.

_____

_____

_____

_____

_____

_____

_____

_____

_____

_____

_____

_____

_____

_____

_____

_____

_____

_____

Notice how you tell your personal story to yourself and others through the way you present yourself, what you think, how you speak, what you say, what you are passionate about, and even what you love and hate.

- PAGE 17 -

Become aware of three examples of how you might begin telling your personal story differently. What do you wish to stop saying because it casts a negative light on you? What do you wish to begin saying to cast a more positive light?

_____

_____

_____

_____

_____

_____

_____

_____

_____

_____

_____

_____

_____

_____

_____

_____

*"I needed to understand and really believe
that telling a new story was about offering
a bigger truth about who I am."*

- PAGE 17 -

What new story will express a bigger truth about who you are?

_____

_____

_____

_____

_____

_____

_____

_____

_____

_____

_____

_____

_____

_____

_____

_____

_____

_____

Finding the open path to the mountaintop is an authentic journey. Through it you will discover who you really are. As you begin to climb the mountain, you will change.

- PAGE 18 -

How do you feel about changing? If it makes you uncomfortable, what kind of support do you need to embrace the climb?

_____

_____

_____

_____

_____

_____

_____

_____

_____

_____

_____

_____

_____

_____

_____

_____

_____

_____

Your view of money and material possessions will
greatly influence the degree and speed at which
you attain mountaintop prosperity.

- PAGE 19 -

How do you view money and material possessions? What old
views and beliefs do you need to let go?

_____

_____

_____

_____

_____

_____

_____

_____

_____

_____

_____

_____

_____

_____

_____

_____

Setting healthy goals from the open path
allows us to live on that surreal plane of reality
that dances with the possible.

- PAGE 21 -

Have you glimpsed that surreal plane of reality that dances with
the possible? How would you describe it?

_____

_____

_____

_____

_____

_____

_____

_____

_____

_____

_____

_____

_____

_____

_____

_____

_____

_____

In realizing that the word hope itself held power,
I understood that it was the ticket to getting
more out of life. I began to lean into hope.

- PAGE 21 -

Describe your level of hope. If it is low, how can you lean into it?

_____

_____

_____

_____

_____

_____

_____

_____

_____

_____

_____

_____

_____

_____

_____

_____

_____

_____

Striving to have the hope of a child and the wisdom of an elder allows us to be patient and strong in our hope.

- PAGE 22 -

Are you patient and strong in your hope? If not, how can you become patient and strong?

_____

_____

_____

_____

_____

_____

_____

_____

_____

_____

_____

_____

_____

_____

_____

_____

_____

_____

Mountaintop prosperity requires fearlessness. This doesn't mean that we don't feel fear—we may feel it very powerfully. It means that we are aware of another part of us that does not feel fear, a part of us that is fearless.

- PAGE 22 -

Are you aware of a fearless part of yourself? Describe this part.

_____
_____
_____
_____
_____
_____
_____
_____
_____
_____
_____
_____
_____
_____
_____
_____
_____
_____

As we take each step, learning about mountaintop prosperity and how to get there, mountaintop messages begin to form. We find ourselves thinking of inspiring ideas to share with others: what we've learned, how we've grown, what we've discovered.

- PAGE 23 -

What inspiring ideas would you like to share with others?

_____

_____

_____

_____

_____

_____

_____

_____

_____

_____

_____

_____

_____

_____

_____

_____

_____

_____

With mountaintop prosperity, your life can be
bigger and brighter than you ever thought possible.

- PAGE 24 -

Describe a life bigger and brighter than you ever thought
possible.

_____

_____

_____

_____

_____

_____

_____

_____

_____

_____

_____

_____

_____

_____

_____

_____

_____

PART I UNDERSTANDING MOUNTAINTOP PROSPERITY	
KEY POINTS **CHAPTER TWO** Avoid Mountaintop Dead Ends	What are Mountaintop Dead Ends? First Mountaintop Dead End: Too Selfish Second Mountaintop Dead End: Too Selfless Third Mountaintop Dead End: Too Self-caring Frustration Isolation Powerlessness Jealousy

Letting go of all selfishness isn't possible (and we don't need to eliminate all selfish tendencies on the open path), but being too selfish means that you are out of control and are overly focused on yourself.

- PAGE 26 -

Have you ever felt out of control and overly focused on yourself? Describe this experience.

_____

_____

_____

_____

_____

_____

_____

_____

_____

_____

_____

_____

_____

_____

_____

_____

_____

Life becomes very narrow when you are only focusing on getting more. Reaching the top of the mountain requires an expanded view of self and life.

- PAGE 26 -

Share an example of an expanded view of self and life.

_____

_____

_____

_____

_____

_____

_____

_____

_____

_____

_____

_____

_____

_____

_____

_____

_____

While it is wonderful to be caring and generous,
being too selfless leads to anger and resentment.

- PAGE 27 -

Have you ever felt angry and resentful because you were too selfless? How can you avoid this dead end?

_____

_____

_____

_____

_____

_____

_____

_____

_____

_____

_____

_____

_____

_____

_____

_____

_____

_____

As you travel up the mountain on the open path,
there will be many opportunities to serve others.

- PAGE 27 -

What are some ways you feel called to serve others that won't
take you to a dead end?

_____

_____

_____

_____

_____

_____

_____

_____

_____

_____

_____

_____

_____

_____

_____

_____

_____

_____

_____

While good self-care is important for everyone,
being too self-caring blocks a vital flow in life.
Being too self-caring keeps your life small.

- PAGE 28 -

Describe an experience of your life being too small due to being too self-caring.

_____

_____

_____

_____

_____

_____

_____

_____

_____

_____

_____

_____

_____

_____

_____

_____

_____

Jealousy is a very toxic emotion; it tells you that you have taken a wrong turn either within yourself or in your life.

- PAGE 29 -

Describe a time when you felt jealous and how it affected your personal energy:

_____

_____

_____

_____

_____

_____

_____

_____

_____

_____

_____

_____

_____

_____

_____

_____

_____

*The answer to all dead ends is breaking through
to the open path. Understanding how to break through
is the key to reaching mountaintop prosperity.*

- PAGE 30 -

How will you remind yourself of the above guidance?

_____

_____

_____

_____

_____

_____

_____

_____

_____

_____

_____

_____

_____

_____

_____

_____

_____

PART I UNDERSTANDING MOUNTAINTOP PROSPERITY	
KEY POINTS **CHAPTER THREE** **Breakthroughs–Eight** **Steps to the Mountaintop**	First Breakthrough: Finding the Open Path Second Breakthrough: Mountaintop Insight Third Breakthrough: Mountaintop Inspiration Fourth Breakthrough: Mountaintop Recognition Fifth Breakthrough: Carrying the Mountaintop Flame Sixth Breakthrough: Mountaintop Resonance Seventh Breakthrough: Mountaintop Streaming Eighth Breakthrough: Mountaintop Identification

*When we are on the open path, we have discovered
our "great latent self." This is the deepest part of us,
which holds the key to the most powerful, loving,
and successful aspects of our being.*

- PAGE 31 -

Describe the most powerful, loving and successful aspects of
your being.

_____

_____

_____

_____

_____

_____

_____

_____

_____

_____

_____

_____

_____

_____

_____

_____

_____

_____

The open path is not about being perfect.
It is about being authentic.

- PAGE 32 -

What does it mean to you to be authentic?

_____

_____

_____

_____

_____

_____

_____

_____

_____

_____

_____

_____

_____

_____

_____

_____

When we break through to mountaintop insight,
our visual perception often shifts. Colors look brighter.
The universe appears to be animated like never before.

- PAGE 33 -

Have you had an experience like the one described in the
passage above? If so, describe it here.

_____

_____

_____

_____

_____

_____

_____

_____

_____

_____

_____

_____

_____

_____

_____

_____

"My pain was no longer that of loss. It suddenly became the pain of birth. My new life was birthing."

- PAGE 34 -

Have you ever had an experience like the one described above? What was your experience?

_____

_____

_____

_____

_____

_____

_____

_____

_____

_____

_____

_____

_____

_____

_____

_____

_____

_____

The third breakthrough to mountaintop inspiration brings a greater sense of well-being. The rising of our great latent self is a strengthening experience.

- PAGE 35 -

Describe a time when you felt a sense of greater well-being. What were the circumstances?

_____

_____

_____

_____

_____

_____

_____

_____

_____

_____

_____

_____

_____

_____

_____

_____

_____

We understand that life is much more mysterious than we had previously thought and that while we are living in the world of ordinary affairs, something extraordinary is happening in our lives.

– PAGE 35 –

Do you relate to the above passage? How?

_____

_____

_____

_____

_____

_____

_____

_____

_____

_____

_____

_____

_____

_____

_____

_____

_____

*With the fifth breakthrough, we are carrying the
mountaintop flame and have fallen in love with life.
We have a heightened appreciation for beauty and a desire
to tell everyone about how incredible life is.*

– PAGE 36 –

Do you relate to the above passage? Give an example of how
you have fallen in love with life.

_____

_____

_____

_____

_____

_____

_____

_____

_____

_____

_____

_____

_____

_____

_____

_____

With the sixth breakthrough,
we develop a mountaintop practice to live
more consciously on every level.

- PAGE 37 -

Do you have a mountaintop practice? Describe it here.

_____

_____

_____

_____

_____

_____

_____

_____

_____

_____

_____

_____

_____

_____

_____

_____

_____

_____

With mountaintop streaming, we optimize our use of time. We always seem to know the next step without even considering it.

- PAGE 38 -

Do you relate to the above passage? Describe an experience of knowing your next step without even considering it.

_____

_____

_____

_____

_____

_____

_____

_____

_____

_____

_____

_____

_____

_____

_____

_____

_____

_____

_____

Through mountaintop identification, we effortlessly
utilize our highest potential in all aspects of our lives.
We have complete trust in ourselves and the universe.

- PAGE 40 -

Do you relate to the above passage? Describe an experience of
trust in yourself and the universe.

_____

_____

_____

_____

_____

_____

_____

_____

_____

_____

_____

_____

_____

_____

_____

_____

"When I remember that I am that big, that great, that amazing,
life is instantly that big, that great, that amazing.
It is not just because I am thinking it so—it really is so.
Things shift and move, and amazing things happen."

- PAGE 40 -

Do you relate to the above passage? Describe some amazing things that have happened in your life.

_____

_____

_____

_____

_____

_____

_____

_____

_____

_____

_____

_____

_____

_____

_____

_____

_____

_____

PART II EMERGING ABOVE THE FOG	
KEY POINTS CHAPTER FOUR Meet Your Great Latent Self	Know the Role of Your Ego
	Identify False Limits
	Unify Your Words and Actions
	Discover Your Self-authority
	A "Round-Up" Practice

Our great latent self holds such remarkable power
that without a commitment to use our power for
mountaintop prosperity, our ego will block it.

- PAGE 45 -

Describe your sense of the power your great latent self holds.

_____

_____

_____

_____

_____

_____

_____

_____

_____

_____

_____

_____

_____

_____

_____

_____

_____

_____

We become imprisoned when our ego rules us,
and it is a prison that can be escaped only
by the great latent self.

- PAGE 46 -

Describe a time when you felt imprisoned by your ego. How can your great latent self free you from that prison?

_____

_____

_____

_____

_____

_____

_____

_____

_____

_____

_____

_____

_____

_____

_____

_____

_____

_____

Identifying our false limits and choosing to move beyond them puts us in the ring to fight for our authentic lives, the lives we want at the mountaintop.

- PAGE 48 -

What are some of your false limits? How will you fight for your authentic life?

_____

_____

_____

_____

_____

_____

_____

_____

_____

_____

_____

_____

_____

_____

_____

_____

_____

_____

Validation is about knowing that the ego
can trick you into taking a dead-end path.
It is about reaching out for support and guidance
when you are unsure.

- PAGE 49 -

Do you reach out for guidance when you are unsure? If not, how can you change this?

_____

_____

_____

_____

_____

_____

_____

_____

_____

_____

_____

_____

_____

_____

_____

_____

_____

_____

*Big gestures. Big smiles. Big laughter. Big animation
of spirit. This is what we recover on the open path.
Our self-authority allows us to live big because
we have defined safe limits for ourselves.*

- PAGE 50 -

Describe what it means for you to live big.

_____

_____

_____

_____

_____

_____

_____

_____

_____

_____

_____

_____

_____

_____

_____

_____

_____

Our great latent self is our loving adult,
our inner adult who will be right there with us
on the open path watching for potential danger.
Our ego can be freed.

- PAGE 50 -

Describe the part of you that you know will be right there
watching for possible danger.

_____

_____

_____

_____

_____

_____

_____

_____

_____

_____

_____

_____

_____

_____

_____

_____

_____

_____

Your great latent self carries a distinct blueprint
of your greatest potential, while your ego
is formed from a standard mold.

- PAGE 51 -

What is your sense of the difference between your distinct
blueprint and the standard mold of the ego?

_____

_____

_____

_____

_____

_____

_____

_____

_____

_____

_____

_____

_____

_____

_____

*As you travel the open path, you will develop
your distinctness and this development holds your
greatest potential to reach the mountaintop.*

- PAGE 51 -

Why does your distinctness hold your greatest potential to reach
the mountaintop?

_____

_____

_____

_____

_____

_____

_____

_____

_____

_____

_____

_____

_____

_____

_____

_____

_____

Train yourself to naturally bring greater
kindness, respect, admiration, and joy
to yourself and others.

- PAGE 52 -

How will you bring greater kindness, respect, admiration, and joy to yourself and others?

_____

_____

_____

_____

_____

_____

_____

_____

_____

_____

_____

_____

_____

_____

_____

_____

_____

_____

PART II EMERGING ABOVE THE FOG	
KEY POINTS **CHAPTER FIVE** **Develop Mountaintop Thinking**	Get Beyond Confusion Balance Your Thoughts Develop Self-confidence Chase Worry Away Strive to Stream Nurture Your Big Ideas

While the ego may slam you with self-doubt, self-shaming,
and self-criticism, you will help your great latent self
break free your ego's hold by giving it a voice.

- PAGE 54 -

What is an example of giving your great latent self a voice? What could it say in response to the ego's hold?

_____

_____

_____

_____

_____

_____

_____

_____

_____

_____

_____

_____

_____

_____

_____

_____

While your ego thinks limiting thoughts,
your great latent self thinks expansively.

- PAGE 55 -

Write three examples of your expansive thoughts.

_____

_____

_____

_____

_____

_____

_____

_____

_____

_____

_____

_____

_____

_____

_____

_____

_____

_____

_____

*Rather than merely increasing our positive thoughts
or trying to eliminate our critical thoughts altogether,
we must balance our thinking.*

- PAGE 55 -

Write an example of your balanced thinking. What does it feel like? How do you act when your thinking is balanced?

_____

_____

_____

_____

_____

_____

_____

_____

_____

_____

_____

_____

_____

_____

_____

_____

_____

_____

_____

_____

With balanced thinking, your critical thoughts
support you. They tell you what is reasonable
and not reasonable for your vision.

- PAGE 56 -

How do your critical thoughts support you?

Your great latent self will always defer to the sphere of genius
by connecting to the higher intelligence in the universe
to keep your life in balance.

- PAGE 56 -

Describe a time when you felt connected to a higher intelligence
in the universe to keep you balanced in life.

_____

_____

_____

_____

_____

_____

_____

_____

_____

_____

_____

_____

_____

_____

_____

_____

_____

_____

To stay on the open path, we must
continually develop our self-confidence.
We must strive to make it stronger.

- PAGE 57 -

Describe ways that you will develop your self-confidence.

_____

_____

_____

_____

_____

_____

_____

_____

_____

_____

_____

_____

_____

_____

_____

_____

_____

_____

_____

*Carry a deep certainty about your great latent self
and the sphere of genius as you live your life in the world,
and watch how your interactions improve without you
uttering a single word.*

- PAGE 58 -

Describe your deep certainty about your great latent self. How
does it support you?

_____

_____

_____

_____

_____

_____

_____

_____

_____

_____

_____

_____

_____

_____

_____

_____

_____

_____

If you are worrying, have a conversation with
your great latent self and listen for a resolution
to your problem that you can hold close to your heart.

- PAGE 59 -

Use the above guidance and write about a conversation with
your great latent self.

_____

_____

_____

_____

_____

_____

_____

_____

_____

_____

_____

_____

_____

_____

_____

_____

_____

_____

At some point, streaming extends beyond a practice.
Streaming becomes a way of life—the new normal.

- PAGE 59 -

Is streaming a new normal for you? How often and under what
circumstances do you stream?

_____

_____

_____

_____

_____

_____

_____

_____

_____

_____

_____

_____

_____

_____

_____

_____

_____

_____

_____

Streaming brings big ideas to us, and big ideas bring about incredible passion, lighting the fire in your belly.

- PAGE 59 -

Do you experience passion that lights a fire in your belly? What are some of the big ideas that come to you while streaming?

_____

_____

_____

_____

_____

_____

_____

_____

_____

_____

_____

_____

_____

_____

_____

_____

_____

_____

_____

Our big ideas lead to big accomplishments, and our big accomplishments lead to greater prosperity.

- PAGE 60 -

Write and example of how a big idea led to a big accomplishment in your life.

_____

_____

_____

_____

_____

_____

_____

_____

_____

_____

_____

_____

_____

_____

_____

_____

_____

PART II EMERGING ABOVE THE FOG	
KEY POINTS CHAPTER SIX Persist Through Challenges	Bumps on the Open Path
	Find Your Footing in Organization
	Meet Challenge with Calm
	Protect Your Drive
	Relish Your Vitality
	Partner with Your Future

When we demonstrate that we will get up when we fall,
our great latent self has greater room to develop us into the
strong being we need to be to reach the mountaintop.

- PAGE 61 -

Describe a time that you rose after failure.

_____

_____

_____

_____

_____

_____

_____

_____

_____

_____

_____

_____

_____

_____

_____

_____

_____

_____

The bumps in life may be like braille
guiding you away from danger and making sure
that you remain true to the path.

- PAGE 62 -

Describe a time when you felt guided away from danger.

_____

_____

_____

_____

_____

_____

_____

_____

_____

_____

_____

_____

_____

_____

_____

_____

_____

_____

Your footing on the open path is determined by how organized you are. When the open path becomes bumpy, increase your level of organization.

- PAGE 63 -

How can you increase your organization in life?

_____

_____

_____

_____

_____

_____

_____

_____

_____

_____

_____

_____

_____

_____

_____

_____

_____

_____

170 | Daphne Michaels

*We need to trim on every level: our possessions,
our communications, our relationships, our paperwork.
A trim and streamlined life is a life that has no limit.*

Describe ways that you can trim your life.

_____

_____

_____

_____

_____

_____

_____

_____

_____

_____

_____

_____

_____

_____

_____

_____

_____

One area where our great latent self can be present but where we seldom invite it to operate is in our daily routines: doing laundry and dishes, grocery shopping, cooking, cleaning, and getting ready for work.

- PAGE 64 -

How is your great latent self present in your daily routines?

_____

_____

_____

_____

_____

_____

_____

_____

_____

_____

_____

_____

_____

_____

_____

_____

_____

_____

Your ego may tell you that your drive is limited,
that you do not have the energy or motivation
for the climb, but your great latent self
possesses a drive that is limitless.

– PAGE 65 –

How would you describe your drive? Are you connecting to your great latent self?

_____

_____

_____

_____

_____

_____

_____

_____

_____

_____

_____

_____

_____

_____

_____

_____

_____

Weariness is a sign that ego
has regained control of your life.

- PAGE 65 -

Do you experience weariness? How can you break the ego's
hold?

_____

_____

_____

_____

_____

_____

_____

_____

_____

_____

_____

_____

_____

_____

_____

_____

_____

_____

_____

High vitality is a sign that we are connected
to our great latent self and the sphere of genius.
Mountaintop prosperity and vitality go hand in hand.
Traveling the open path gives us greater vitality.

- PAGE 66 -

Describe your level of vitality. How can you increase it?

_____

_____

_____

_____

_____

_____

_____

_____

_____

_____

_____

_____

_____

_____

_____

_____

_____

_____

When we relish our vitality, challenges on the
open path are not insurmountable. We become confident
that we can resolve the issues that arise.

- PAGE 67 -

Describe how greater vitality creates greater confidence.

_____

_____

_____

_____

_____

_____

_____

_____

_____

_____

_____

_____

_____

_____

_____

_____

_____

_____

Let the spirit of your future pull you toward
greater prosperity. Be all in.

- PAGE 67 -

Are you "all in" on the open path? How can you allow the spirit of your future to pull you toward mountaintop prosperity?

_____

_____

_____

_____

_____

_____

_____

_____

_____

_____

_____

_____

_____

_____

_____

_____

_____

_____

With your great latent self present to decode messages from your challenges, you will be amazed at how quickly your challenges resolve and how ingenious the resolutions will be.

- PAGE 68 -

Write about two examples of challenges resolving in ingenious ways in your life.

_____

_____
_____
_____
_____
_____
_____
_____
_____
_____
_____
_____
_____
_____
_____
_____
_____
_____
_____
_____

PART II EMERGING ABOVE THE FOG	
KEY POINTS CHAPTER SEVEN Develop a Triumphant Approach	Understand Mountaintop Security Recall Past Triumphs Get and Stay Unstuck Cultivate Your Strengths Commit to the Open Path Aspire to Excellence Believe in Your Great Latent Self

A triumphant approach is about giving yourself credit for putting one foot in front of the other in climbing the mountain, knowing there may be wins and losses along the way. The real win is that you remain on the open path.

- PAGE 69-70 -

Describe how you give yourself credit for remaining on the open path.

_____

_____

_____

_____

_____

_____

_____

_____

_____

_____

_____

_____

_____

_____

_____

_____

_____

_____

_____

Ego is the maker of all resistance. Its apathy and paralysis can be incredibly powerful, so much so that it can keep us stuck for an entire lifetime.

- PAGE 71 -

How resistant are you to the open path? How can you reduce your resistance?

_____

_____

_____

_____

_____

_____

_____

_____

_____

_____

_____

_____

_____

_____

_____

_____

_____

_____

*Develop a habit of saying yes. While ego's favorite
word is no, the great latent self's favorite word is yes!
Look for opportunities to say yes, and say yes more often.*

- PAGE 73 -

List the last five times you said yes. Are there more opportunities
to say yes?

_____

_____

_____

_____

_____

_____

_____

_____

_____

_____

_____

_____

_____

_____

_____

_____

_____

_____

Developing our strength is not about
wishing and hoping. It is about the actual,
real development of our being.

- PAGE 73 -

How do you develop your strengths?

_____

_____

_____

_____

_____

_____

_____

_____

_____

_____

_____

_____

_____

_____

_____

_____

A triumphant approach means striving to surpass ordinary standards. When we strive for excellence, we are allowing our great latent self to be more present in our life and show us what we are really capable of.

- PAGE 76 -

List three things that your great latent self is showing you that you are capable of?

_____

_____

_____

_____

_____

_____

_____

_____

_____

_____

_____

_____

_____

_____

_____

_____

PART II EMERGING ABOVE THE FOG	
KEY POINTS **CHAPTER EIGHT** Stoke the Fire in Your Belly	Use Your Mountaintop Memory Embrace Your Mountaintop Desires See Yourself on the Mountaintop Direct Your Mountaintop Passion Celebrate Mountaintop Success Clarify Your Mountaintop Goals Keep Your Mountaintop Spark Alive

Passion taps into your personal energy in a timeless way.
By recalling a past passion, you have access
to that personal energy right now.

- PAGE 79 -

Recall a past passion and describe how it taps into your personal energy now.

_____

_____

_____

_____

_____

_____

_____

_____

_____

_____

_____

_____

_____

_____

_____

_____

_____

_____

_____

When your desires come from your great latent self,
they are deep desires. They have power and
potency and meaning.

- PAGE 81 -

Describe three desires that have power and potency and
meaning.

_____

_____

_____

_____

_____

_____

_____

_____

_____

_____

_____

_____

_____

_____

_____

_____

_____

*Allow your desires to become your map on the open path.
They are a reflection of you, and embracing them will
prepare you to embrace the joys and pleasures ahead.*

- PAGE 81 -

What desires are your map?

_____

_____

_____

_____

_____

_____

_____

_____

_____

_____

_____

_____

_____

_____

_____

_____

_____

_____

*Each mountaintop success, regardless of how
large or small it is, must be celebrated.*

- PAGE 83 -

How have you celebrated your last two mountaintop successes?

Hold the intention of keeping your mountaintop spark alive.
Build your capacity to keep it alive. Use your triumphant
approach to keep it alive. Do whatever you need to do
to keep your spark glowing.

- PAGE 86 -

How will you keep your mountaintop spark alive?

_____

_____

_____

_____

_____

_____

_____

_____

_____

_____

_____

_____

_____

_____

_____

_____

_____

_____

PART III	
LIVING MOUNTAINTOP PROSPERITY	
KEY POINTS CHAPTER NINE Surrender to the Highest Good	Surrender Through Curiosity
	Our Amphibious Nature
	Trust is Our Birthright
	The Magic of Momentum
	Stay on the Creative Wave
	The Glow of Surrender
	Watch Your Life Unfold

We surrender to the highest good when
we surrender to our curiosity. We no longer
need to have all the answers.

- PAGE 89 -

Do you relate to the above passage? What does it mean in
your life?

_____

_____

_____

_____

_____

_____

_____

_____

_____

_____

_____

_____

_____

_____

_____

_____

_____

_____

Our amphibious nature allows us to be both steadfast in our approach and fluid when flexibility is needed.

- PAGE 90 -

Describe how you are steadfast in your life and how you are fluid.

_____

_____

_____

_____

_____

_____

_____

_____

_____

_____

_____

_____

_____

_____

_____

_____

_____

_____

Trust is like a golden thread of purity,
and it carries the spark of life.

- PAGE 91 -

Describe your capacity to trust. How can you increase your trust in life?

_____

_____

_____

_____

_____

_____

_____

_____

_____

_____

_____

_____

_____

_____

_____

_____

_____

_____

_____

_____

On the creative wave, we can have more—more money,
more friendship, more engagement with life, more fun,
more meaning, more of whatever we choose.

- PAGE 92 -

How have you used your creativity to gain more in your life?

_____

_____

_____

_____

_____

_____

_____

_____

_____

_____

_____

_____

_____

_____

_____

_____

_____

When our great latent self is present, it animates our being.
The sphere of genius shines through us. We take on
a childlike vitality regardless of our age.

- PAGE 92 -

How do you take on a childlike vitality?

_____

_____

_____

_____

_____

_____

_____

_____

_____

_____

_____

_____

_____

_____

_____

_____

_____

PART III LIVING MOUNTAINTOP PROSPERITY	
KEY POINTS CHAPTER TEN Cultivate Your Courage to Love	Mountaintop Prosperity is Love
	Mountaintop Love is a Glue
	Mountaintop Love is a Motivator
	Aspiration is Mountaintop Self-love
	Recover Pure Mountaintop Love
	Turn Grudges into Mountaintop Gratitude
	Mountaintop Love and Prosperity

"My love extends to everything.
I have discovered mountaintop love."

- PAGE 96 -

Have you discovered mountaintop love? Describe your
experience.

_____

_____

_____

_____

_____

_____

_____

_____

_____

_____

_____

_____

_____

_____

_____

_____

_____

_____

Whenever the great latent self is free from the ego,
an orbit of love is created. Our lives
naturally move into order.

- PAGE 97 -

Describe a time when being free from your ego naturally moved
your life into order.

_____

_____

_____

_____

_____

_____

_____

_____

_____

_____

_____

_____

_____

_____

_____

_____

_____

The truth is that aspiration is mountaintop self-love,
a type of love that honors life itself.

- PAGE 98 -

Describe how your aspirations are self-love.

_____

_____

_____

_____

_____

_____

_____

_____

_____

_____

_____

_____

_____

_____

_____

_____

_____

_____

"I got a glimpse of what self-love is all about.
It was about going after the life I really wanted."

- PAGE 98 -

Describe what it would look like to go after the life you really
want.

_____

_____

_____

_____

_____

_____

_____

_____

_____

_____

_____

_____

_____

_____

_____

_____

_____

We are made to survive loss.
We are not made to live without love.
Our task on the mountaintop is to recover
our ability to love and to recover it fully.

- PAGE 99 -

Describe what it means to you to recover your ability to love fully.

_____

_____

_____

_____

_____

_____

_____

_____

_____

_____

_____

_____

_____

_____

_____

_____

_____

_____

PART III LIVING MOUNTAINTOP PROSPERITY	
KEY POINTS **CHAPTER ELEVEN** **Embrace the World**	We Are in It Together Why Your Charisma Matters Mountaintop Collaboration

*Manifesting mountaintop prosperity
requires that you put one foot in front of the other,
and it takes a commitment to the open path.*

- PAGE 103 -

Describe your commitment to the open path.

In this mountaintop togetherness
are the answers to the world's problems
that we will never find alone.

- PAGE 103 -

What does the above passage mean to you?

_____

_____

_____

_____

_____

_____

_____

_____

_____

_____

_____

_____

_____

_____

_____

_____

_____

_____

Mountaintop streaming in community is our next task,
a great new mountain with a great new peak.
Discovering a new message about the world
on this new mountain is our new task.

- PAGE 104 -

What do you imagine the new message about the world on this new mountain to be?

_____

_____

_____

_____

_____

_____

_____

_____

_____

_____

_____

_____

_____

_____

_____

_____

_____

_____

Acknowledgments

Thank you to all of the committed, courageous, and tenacious women and men I've worked with over the years. It has been such a joy to watch you climb to your mountaintops!

I am extremely fortunate to have had a top-of-the line independent publishing team support me throughout the creation of Mountaintop Prosperity. Many thanks to:

Lead Consultant: Bruce McAllister

Interior Page Designer: Jerry Henness

Content Organization and Transcription: Ann McIndoo

Writing, Editing and Publishing Consultants: Martha Bullen, Debbie Englander, and Geoffrey Berwind

Publicity Experts: Steve Harrison, Virginia Sheppard, Danette Kubanda, Mary Guissefi, and Stacy Rollins

Editor: Sandi Corbitt-Sears

Cover Designer: George Foster

A special thank-you to Marci Shimoff and Janet Bray Attwood for your beautiful endorsements.

To my son, Gabriel: Your pure heart inspires me to teach others about the open path through my mountaintop message!

About the Author

Daphne Michaels is a leading expert in guiding others to their highest potential. As a speaker, author and trainer, she has helped thousands of people for more than 20 years, and is a pioneer in the field of how tapping personal energy improves daily life. Her life-long journey includes formal training in the social sciences and integral psychology and rewarding work as a licensed psychotherapist and executive consultant.

Forthcoming Books

Luxurious You: *Move Beyond Your Fear of Greatness for a Mountaintop Life*

Open Path: *Breakthrough to Mountaintop Excellence*

Contact Daphne Michaels

For more information and to schedule Daphne Michaels for:
• Keynote Speaking
• Corporate Training
• Consulting
• Mentoring

Email: info@daphnemichaels.com
Website: daphnemichaels.com
Facebook: facebook.com/daphnemichaelsbooks
Twitter: twitter.com/daphne_michaels
Linkedin: linkedin.com/in/daphnemichaels

Discover Your Next Mountaintop Move

Be part of the MOUNTAINTOP MOVEMENT!

Great success demands that you have a compass; a place within to regroup and decide — in an instant — which direction to move. You must have clarity — for cutting edge influence, to achieve complex missions, to win bottom line negotiations, and to build productive long-term relationships.

The MOUNTAINTOP MOVEMENT is about you achieving great success by becoming an extraordinary person; one with an inner compass. It means knowing how to live life with greater insight, inspiration and intelligence.

As a leading expert in helping people excel, in life and work, I invite you to work with me and learn proven methods to move quickly to new heights in *your* life.

My goal is for you to always know your next mountaintop move. Learn more today: daphnemichaels.com